A
Memoir

Amoghavajra

A MEMOIR

AMOGHAVAJRA

ISBN 978-0-244-84994-8

SECOND EDITION 2020

COPYRIGHT © AMOGHAVAJRA (KENNETH MACKAY)

THE AUTHOR'S MORAL RIGHTS HAVE BEEN ASSERTED.

ALL RIGHTS RESERVED.

FRONT COVER BY JOHN G LAMMIE.

ABOUT THE AUTHOR

Amoghavajra was ordained into the Triratna Buddhist Order in 1982, and lives in Ipswich, UK. He was Chairman of the Ipswich Buddhist Centre for many years. A wheelchair-user, he has been an International Wheelchair Basketball Federation 'classifier' and tutor and was active in the London and Beijing Paralympics.

CONTENTS

Prologue	6
Life is nothing, if not an adventure	9
My two 'families'	11
A Journey to the West Highlands	12
Gairloch beckons	17
A wedding in Glasgow	20
And on to University	21
Going South to the 'sensuous land of beauty'	22
And then this happens…	25
Intensive Care Unit	27
Dad arrives!	30
Another Existential crisis!	31
Finding the Dharma in Glasgow – The jewel in the dung-heap!	35
Our first night	38
Listening to Sangharakshita give a talk	39
Vibrancy and energy	40
My friend Andrew becomes Susiddhi	41
The wider FWBO world – another new beginning, and an ending	43
A Buddhist Centre in Bethnal Green	44
Meeting Sangharakshita	45
A painful parting	49
My first retreat	51
A stillness that vibrated and hummed	53
A meditation master	55

THE RETREAT ENDS, ALL THINGS CHANGE, RETURNING TO THE WORLD	58
UNIVERSITY CONTINUES	59
SEXUALITY AND DISABILITY MEETS CALVINISM!	60
MY CAREER GOES DOWN THE PLUGHOLE	63
MY INTEREST IN BUDDHISM DEEPENS	65
THOSE EARLY SANGHA MEMBERS	67
AND THE ORDER MEMBERS - BRIGHT FREE AND DYNAMIC!	68
OPEN COMMUNICATION	71
HEADING SOUTH AGAIN	74
MY FIRST CAR	76
GRADUATION	78
MY SECOND RETREAT – LOCH SUNART	81
RIGHT LIVELIHOOD – INK PRINT & DESIGN	86
HERUKA – MEN'S COMMUNITY	89
HOUSING AND MY FAMILY HOME	89
WHEELCHAIR ACCESSIBLE ACCOMMODATION	94
REFURBISHING 102 CARTSIDE STREET	94
PARENTS	95
LEAVING HOME	98
13 KELVINSIDE SOUTH	100
GOING FORTH	102
LIVING IN THE COMMUNITY	104
DAILY ROUTINE	106
CLOSED COMMUNITY AND FRIENDSHIP	107
OPENNESS	108
COMMON PURSE	109
DISABILITY AND SEXUALITY	111

Prologue

Half a dozen of us had taken a break from our business meeting to have afternoon tea with our Buddhist teacher and guide – Sangharakshita. He was now in his 80's and although no longer the sole guiding figure he had been, he still kept a keen interest in what was going on around the Buddhist movement he had founded in the 1960s. This was around 2014 when I was Chair of the Ipswich Buddhist Centre and also part of the Exec that helped manage the business of the Triratna European Chairs Assembly.

As a young man in pre-WWII London Sangharakshita had come across Buddhism via the Diamond Sutra and realised that he was, and had always been, a Buddhist. This was remarkable enough for these times, but then he had the good fortune to find himself in India, the homeland of the Buddha. Conscripted into the army towards the end of the war, he was posted to India. After leaving the army, he spent some time as a homeless wanderer before being ordained as a Buddhist monk. He became a disciple of Jagdish Kasyap in Benares. Then he went on tour with his teacher to Nepal. Kasyap left him in Kalimpong with the injunction 'To work for the good of Buddhism in Kalimpong.' This was the time when many Tibetan refugees were fleeing the Chinese invasion and persecution in their homeland. Many of those refugees were high ranking Buddhist lamas and they were coming through Kalimpong on their way to freedom in the West. Some of these teachers responded well to this young English monk and began to teach and mentor him. Sangharakshita himself was becoming a prolific writer - editing magazines, writing up his talks and publishing his own 'Survey of Buddhism'. On returning to London in the 1960s he started a new Buddhist movement that then spread from its London roots to many cities across the UK and then worldwide. He led numerous retreats and seminars, gave talks and continued to write profusely and publish many more books and commentaries on the Buddhist sacred texts. He was a spiritual tour-de-force.

Sangharakshita now lived in a leafy suburb of Birmingham where he had gathered his senior disciples. It was in this grand, detached Victorian building that we had been meeting to co-ordinate Centre activities of this Buddhist movement. These were long days of discussion and an afternoon break was welcome. Especially if it involved time with such a creative, productive, deep thinker. These occasions also had an air of frisson as Sangharakshita could be very forthright, direct and uncompromising in his communication. Engaging with him could be 'dangerous' in this respect.

At 4 p.m. we gathered around the large bay window in a room overlooking the lush garden. Sangharakshita joined us from his annexe and we settled down to our afternoon tea. Sangharakshita enquired what business we had been discussing. One of the areas we had been discussing had been the publishing of new books in different styles, by order members of different standing in our Order. Sangharakshita always took a keen interest in books as he was an avid reader and knew how important books could be in communicating life-changing ideas. These meetings with Sangharakshita always went better if someone was able to draw him out a bit more, get Sangharakshita to elucidate some of his thinking. In an attempt to do this one of our number asked

'Bhante, who do you think should write.' (Bhante is a Buddhist term of respect.)

'Aah.' he said and pondered for a microsecond. Then lifted the index finger of his right hand and extending it in my direction he said 'You.'.

I felt seen. I felt exposed. Gently challenged. That 3-letter word penetrated my heart and lodged there. As much as an opportunity, as a challenge.

But what could I write, I wasn't a clear thinker or a poet. The only thing I thought I could write about was my life.

A few years later, when I had moved on from some major responsibilities and had free time, I turned my mind to that challenging request. And so, this memoir, which had been germinating in my heart since that afternoon, was born.

Amoghavajra.
3rd January 2020,
Ipswich.

Life is Nothing, if not an Adventure

We were sitting on the Post Bus as it pulled away from the train station. The view was open and expansiveness, revealing a vast empty moor edged with mountains all around. And so much sky. And magnificent beauty. Apart from the station there were precious few other houses or cottages around to explain why the train stopped here. Just a road junction. And both roads seemed to head into the oblivion of the moor. And you just trusted that the road would find a way through this impenetrable ring of rock. The junction offered two choices : south to Kyle of Lochalsh or west to Ullapool. We went west.

Aultbea is a small village on the eastern shore of Loch Ewe, nearly 250 miles north of Glasgow. Loch Ewe is the only north-facing loch in Scotland and lies in Wester Ross in the West Highlands. The village of Aultbea strings itself along the shoreline for a mile or more. Behind the village lies an open uninhabited expanse of moor and bog, occasionally surprised by lochs, lochans and hills. The elements of sea, sky and earth hold dominion here like the Grandmasters they are. The vast Atlantic Ocean opens up before you. Not much lies between here and the Americas, except thousands of miles of watery depths. The locals have become expert at sailing these dangerous waters in search of food and commerce. Above you, circling these skies, is the realm of the Golden Eagle whose wingspan is equal to the height of a tall man. The winds in these parts coming straight off the sea where their strength has been unopposed across the expanse of the ocean. You feel the weight behind you of a towering landscape stretching inward, mountains of ancient Lewisian Gneiss reach to the sky. The theatre of man is dwarfed by these indiscriminate elements. In Glasgow the elements have largely been tamed, and the violence human. Here in Wester Ross the unruliness of humanity is dwarfed by these indiscriminate elements that dominate life. Here I would be away from the violence and heaviness of 1970s Glasgow, away from an urban life in a northern European city.

Me and my best friend Johnny Walker had decided to find work during the summer before starting University. We had known each other well since our first days in Primary School. We were both quite bright academically, had played football together, and hung out a lot. After Primary we had gone to different fee-paying schools, but even that experience had brought us together. As neither of us had gone to the local secondary, we both had this experience of being a bit different. He went to Allan Glens'; I went to Glasgow High School. We went dancing together, looking for girlfriends, had found Saturday jobs together, and liked similar music.

We had heard that you could find summer work easily in hotels. So, Johnny and I had gone to a Catering Job Agency in Bath Street to look for work. On their list was a hotel in Wester Ross where our agent thought we would find work. A short phone call had confirmed that the hotel was still looking for staff. We took the job on the recommendation of our agent and began to plan our journey. The immediacy of the telephone call to Aultbea belied the distance between Glasgow and Wester Ross.

A week later we were sitting on a post bus pulling out of Achnasheen. This was after a long train journey to Inverness, then another train to Achnasheen. At Achnasheen we picked up this Post Bus that would take us the last leg of the trip to Aultbea. The Post Bus delivers and picks up mail as well as its human passengers, and wasn't much bigger than a Ford Transit van. Achnasheen is so small it hardly deserves a name to distinguish it, just a few cottages and houses. We were soon out of this small hamlet travelling on a road that hugged a small highland loch. Then we lost this body of water as we climbed over a high pass. Ahead we could see high mountains scraping clouds in the sky. And the road climbed higher. As we began to drop the winding road revealed another shimmering of water ahead. Loch Maree has many small isles on it that appear to float on its surface. The Scots pine growing on the isles contribute a sense of awe – how can trees have their roots in water! The northern side of the loch is dominated by high, bleak, grey mountains that block any distant view. Past Slattadale the road climbs away from Loch Maree and is befriended by smaller lochs and lochans on either side of the road. This is a bleak and barren beauty. The road is accompanied by a stream, and both tumble down a ravine. Until we arrive at the sea loch at the village of Gairloch. Where the land becomes fertile and green once more, and you remember gratefully how bountiful nature can be. Sometimes the road is single-tracked with the occasional passing place bulging out the side. A little climb as the road turns away from the sea and then another descent into another loch. This time it is Loch Broom that stretches away to our north.

Seven miles along this scenic road the driver lets us off the bus, just before Aultbea. There is a steep walk up the brae to the Drumchork Lodge. Asking for our directions gives us away as Glaswegians. The locals pronounce the Lodge as Drummahorr. We were as alien to the language as we were to the landscape.

My two 'families'

This journey to the North West was mythical as well as geographical. My father was fostered, and I never knew any grandparents on his side of the family. I had visited my other

Gran in Dennistoun regularly on Sundays when I was small. Around late morning all five siblings and our mother, would traipse down to the bus stop at the foot of the road and get on board the #22 bus. I enjoyed this journey into my mother's family amid the East End of Glasgow. We would get off as the bus turned into Duke Street and walk up Craigpark and turn right into Golfhill Drive. There was a mixture of sixties flats and earlier red sandstone tenements. My Gran and Aunt Isobella lived on the first floor of the tenement at 82. It was a spacious flat for two people with a rather weighty atmosphere. Reached via the typical Glasgow 'close'. The kitchen overlooked the 'back close' at the back of the building and whenever me and my brothers got bored we would escape down into the garden to play.

Although I knew my Mum's three sisters and their families fairly well, I never met or heard much about my father's family. I knew he was brought up in Muir of Ord near Inverness and heard him talk of the croft in Wester Ross where his foster brother still lived with his wife and two children. Every Christmas or New Year we talked briefly with them on the phone, wishing each other well for the coming year and recognizing that another year had passed and gone. I could hear the Highland lilt in their voices and could only imagine much more. Ally's wife, Morag, came from Scalpay, a small island lying just off the Inner Hebridean isle of Harris. So, while I was very familiar with my Glasgow family, my Highland family were much more mysterious. I was one part a deeply rooted Glaswegian, and another part dispossessed Highlander.

A Journey to the West Highlands

The road to Aultbea was the legendary road to the Isles from Inverness to Skye. So, getting off the train at Achnasheen, which was little more than a junction of two old Thomas Telford roads, I could imagine my attention being caught by two gentlemen striding into the coffee shop in what looked like fancy dress. Kilts and tartan hose, blue bonnets, a single white cockade on the brims and what looked like real claymores in their belts and daggers protruding from their socks. "I landed off a French Frigate on Eriskay with seven loyal companions to rout the German Pretender. The men of Knoydart greeted me just like the Prince I am. To a man they had been out in '15 with my father the King against that upstart George of Hanover. Now I have you with me, Murray, our true Jacobite cause, blessed by the Pope himself, is bound to succeed."

Drumchork Lodge was a small hotel and it wasn't busy, especially at lunchtime when we might only have to serve one or two tables. Even at breakfast and evening meal, when it was at its busiest, all the tables would not be occupied. We learned to wait the tables, learned how to interact successfully with the fiery chefs. Began to manage the double swing doors that protected the diners from seeing what actually went on in the kitchen, and thereby saved their appetite. The double swing doors took a bit of getting used to: shouldering open the first and then the second while carrying four or five plates required deft manoeuvring that wasn't always successful. One time while delivering fish, chips and peas, one of Johnnie's fish went tumbling off one plate only to be caught by my good self as I scampered behind him. A quick return to the kitchen to redistribute the fish, and we were back out to deliver. A class act!

We served three meals a day, although lunch was fairly quiet. Apart from serving, we would also set up the tables for the next meal once the diners had left. Able at these moments, with no punters, to indulge in our choice of music – 10cc and 'I'm not in

Love.' being a favourite. Aultbea is very remote and small. We began to get to know staff at the Aultbea Hotel which was much bigger than our hotel. We would go round to visit them in our time off and listen to music. On days off we could explore the area.

One day off we caught the early Post Bus to Laide which was on the North side of the small peninsula. After the ten minute journey to Laide, we got off at the Post Office, which also doubled up as the only shop. Facing North East, Laide had a very different view from Aultbea. We could see North to the Assynt mountains piercing the sky. Later we would hear their evocative Gaelic names - Coigach, Caorach, and further north to Stac Pollaidh, Qinaig, and Col Mor. We were fortunate that our day off was warm and sunny and the sky was cloud-free. We wound our way down to the rocky shore and begin to explore the rock pools left behind by the receding tide. We had brought our swimming gear and I was tempted by the clear blue waters in the rocky bay. I stripped off and plunged in. The cold waters took my breath away, they had looked so inviting, and yet were so cold. On entering the beautiful but icy cold water my body went into shock and I instinctively curled into a ball. I had to struggle to open up from this ball to swim back to the side and climb out. Taking as few strokes as I could, in my rush to get out.

Johnny had been watching my time in the tempting water and enquired

"What is it like?"

"Beautiful," I replied.

Hoping to get some compensation for my own shocking experience by the discomfort of my friend. A bit of youthful schadenfreude. Sharing the shock of the icy sea might make it slightly more bearable. I watched in anticipation as Johnny, now changed into his swimming trunks chose his spot to dive in. I encouraged him, "You'll love it."

Being careful with his foot grip not to slip or slide on the sharp rocks he poised, prepared himself, and then sprung into the air and into the clear blue waters. I watched as he went into the straight line of a perfect dive, fully extended from fingers to toes. Entering the water, he immediately curled into a tight contracted ball of the foetal position. And I confess I smiled at the sight. Knowing that we shared the shocking experience of these icy cold waters, freezing even on a warm sunny day like this. Wondering in awe at the body's immediate instinctive response to the cold water. Like me before him, he immediately turned around, grabbed the nearest rocks and pulled himself out. Our friendship survived this incident, as this was the type of challenging rough and tumble we expected of one another. Typically Glaswegian, without much gentleness, but enjoying the robust game-playing of our 'friendship'.

That summer we visited places with exotic Gaelic names, all within a few miles of Aultbea – Mellon Charles, Bualnaluib, Ormiscraig and Gruinard. At Gruinard we hadn't been able to get onto the small island. In 1942 the British military scientists had tested anthrax as a possible biological weapon on the small island just offshore. This sheltered part of the mainland is green and forested, which makes it quite beautiful, in comparison to some other nearby moors that are rocky and only able to grow the hardy bracken and a kind of marram grass. The island of Gruinard itself was deadly, as the anthrax spores were still live and it was prohibited to land there. It would be another twenty-five years before it was decontaminated and safe to land on.

There were discos in Aultbea at the weekend, but they were not very busy. The best ones were held each Friday in Gairloch at the village hall. So, one Friday Johnny, myself and Martin (a waiter from Bradford) all piled into the car belonging to the son of the hotel owner. This short 12 mile car trip was harrowing. The locals drive fast. Familiar with the local roads, and having long got bored with this beautiful scenery, they just want to get to where they are going. Irritated by the miles of tarmac to the next village they tear up these distances. We did arrive safely, if slightly shaken up, and parked up by the village hall. But first off, we went down the road to the pub in the local hotel. There we had a couple of pints of Tenants lager to loosen off the trials of work. Then off to the dancing in the village hall. We paid our entrance at the door and were happy to be back in a familiar dance world. Loud disco pop and flashing lights, made all the merrier by the few lagers. We had brought our flares and platform shoes just in case, and we weren't disappointed as we strutted our stuff.

The locals seemed to prefer drinking over dancing, and soon got bored of the 'jigging'- as we say in Glasgow. Our lift left early with Johnny and Martin, but I decided to stay on. It was a straight, if long, walk back to Aultbea, along the A832, and I thought I could hardly get lost. There was only the main road here. On the journey down, I had noticed a couple of lochans by the side of the road that seemed so magical that they must be inhabited by Selkies or seal people, the Gaelic mythical mermaids. There was the village of Poolewe halfway back to Aultbea. I was sure I would find my way if I remembered these landmarks.

The disco finished just after midnight, and it was then that I stepped out into the Highland summer night and began to make my way home. Once out of the village the light pollution dropped to almost zero and the stars emerged into the night sky in multitudes. The inky blue sky was awash with hosts of stars, I couldn't ever remember seeing so many. There was enough light from the small moon and the stars to see where I was going. Although in midsummer, on a clear night, it never really gets that dark here in the far north.

The road rose up out of Gairloch and after a wee while I noticed one of the lochans on my right. Then I dropped down into Poolewe, with not a soul in sight. Upwards again out of this village, another lochan this time again on my right. My legs were beginning to tire and my feet felt sore from walking in my 3" platforms shoes. So, I took off my socks and shoes and carried on. Around 4am as the light dawned to grey for the new day, I was on the crest of the hill looking down on Aultbea in the distance. The waters of Loch Ewe extended out before me to my left. Enjoying this full view of the loch and knowing that I was close to home, I felt slightly ecstatic. I had walked through the night in this awesome landscape. A wee while later I got back to the hotel. As I pushed open the door of our shared bedroom, Johnny turned over slightly and moaned a welcome. So, just as Saturday was starting I slipped into my own bed and slept soundly.

GAIRLOCH BECKONS

After a few weeks at the Drumchork Lodge we began to find Aultbea a bit too quiet. We decided to move on to Gairloch which was a bigger place with more nightlife; and Johnny had found out that they were looking for waiters in the Gairloch Hotel.

Although both places were villages in the north-west of Scotland they felt quite different. The view from Gairloch was to the South and particularly stunning. There in the distance we could see the towering ancient peaks of the Torridon Mountains.

We hoped to meet interesting characters from around the world doing this type of work. Seasonal hotel work attracted a number of different types: there were the local people who drifted towards this easy but low-paid work, there were the travellers who enjoyed moving around the country living on the edges of society, and there were the professional staff the chefs and Managers.

The move to Gairloch Hotel brought us into contact with many of these travellers mentioned above as there were more staff needed for this bigger hotel. I remember one beautiful auburn-haired German girl who exuded mystery and the exotic for me. One evening a lot of us decided to go down to the beach in front of the hotel after work finished. Summer evenings in the north of Scotland never get completely dark. And the sky remains a lovely deep dark blue colour even in the middle of the night. The sun lies just below the horizon and at this point the sky is a lighter blue. As we gathered around our bonfire I spoke with Katherine and she introduced me to the novel that she was reading at the moment. It was Steppenwolf by Herman Hesse. This was like a muse introducing me to fine culture. As we spoke I remembered a dream that I had the night before, and in this dream, I was with Katherine and some others down on the beach beside a bonfire! And now here we were gathering beside the bonfire and talking just as had happened in my dream. And so, a quite unusual feeling descended on me. The allure of the evening was swollen by a glimpse of her pale breast in the moonlight as she got undressed, ready for a skinny dip in the sea. This all seemed like high Romance to me.

There were many other interesting characters working there at the hotel. Callum was the hotel electrician. Born on the island of Skye which was visible just to the south. He was a very down to earth and practical man, and although brought up on the remote island he was also quite urbane in his manners. Certainly not a country bumpkin. Whenever I met him, I could almost hear the Jacobite folk songs of my childhood evoking the tales of Bonnie Prince Charlie escaping over the sea, rescued by his loyal Flora Macdonald. Callum spoke with a western lilt in his voice, and told magical tales of his home island.

The whole scene at Gairloch was just what I had been searching for. Here was a colourful world beyond the grey Glasgow I had grown up in. My sense of Glasgow had been one of harshness, and a real mixed response to pleasure, that sense of "if it's sunny today we will pay for it tomorrow". And then there was the gang violence that I had to negotiate. That summer in the magnificent Highlands, life began to open for me and offer something that I was very curiously seeking.

The work at Gairloch was quite different from Drumchork. This time I was in the kitchen, initially as a kitchen porter then dishwashing. I actually enjoyed the work as a dishwasher. It was solitary work, and there was plenty of overtime. Given that there was little else to do I didn't mind working long hours, and I was saving money. Being based in the kitchen meant that I got to know all the kitchen staff pretty well. There were a handful of chefs in the kitchen - sous chefs and pastry chefs as well as the main chef. The heat of the kitchen work was reflected in the fiery temperament of the main chef who didn't suffer fools gladly and it was dangerous to get on the wrong side of them.

The aforementioned Callum told me he had survived a dangerous incident. One day during a thunder and lightning storm he had been working in the back stairway that the staff used to descend from their bedrooms to the working area. A bolt of lightning had shot in the window and earthed itself on the copper pipe just by his arm. He took me to the spot on the staircase and showed me the dark black mark caused by the lightning burning the paint. Then rolled up his shirt sleeve to reveal a mark on his forearm. He had survived the incident relatively unscathed. Whether this was a tale of history or one of his yarns, it was difficult to tell, as he was completely straightforward about it.

A WEDDING IN GLASGOW

After a couple of weeks in Gairloch I was due to return to Glasgow for my sister's wedding. I was to be away for a few days. It was quite a personal milestone seeing my sister moving into a very different phase in her life. Marrying, home-owning and starting work as a PE teacher. My Uncle Ally and Aunt Morag came down from Muir of Ord for the wedding. It was a delight to see them, and to know that they valued their connection with us. Coming to the wedding involved a weekend stay in Glasgow due to the distance. Alan and Shona, my cousins, also came. Fiona and Paul were married at the Glasgow University chapel, and the reception afterwards was at a hotel in Park Circus. At one point in the reception proceedings I heard some singing coming from one of the rooms. Intrigued, I went in to see my Aunt Morag sitting on a dining chair in the middle of the room singing a Gaelic working song unaccompanied. Gaelic women had made up songs with rhythms and words that suited the various tasks given to them. The rhythms kept up their energy as the job was accomplished. For some tasks all the women of the village would gather and work and sing together. I was enchanted by my aunt's singing, she held her audience spellbound, sitting there in her own stillness, hands folded on her lap, singing this song with such precision and vigour. As the song progressed the rhythm became faster and faster, and my aunt kept the pronunciation precise and clear as ever, her foot tapping out the quickening beat. Unknown to me she had sung Puirt-a-beul like this at some of the Mods that were held to keep alive these old traditions.

Back in Gairloch after the wedding I found that Johnny had left and returned to Glasgow. He had become restless and unsettled and taken to drink. It seemed that the remote environment didn't suit him and he had left. I also found that the small sum of money I had been gathering, had been taken from my room. I felt a little betrayed by these events, but stayed on in Gairloch.

Late one morning, a couple of weeks after the wedding, I was called to the hotel's reception. I was stunned to see my Uncle Ally and my two younger brothers Robin and Duncan. Robin and Duncan were on holiday at Muir of Ord at my uncle's croft. It turned out that Ally worked on the roads for Wester Ross Council and knew this area well. They had surprised me by driving the sixty miles from Muir of Ord to Gairloch to visit. In my mind I was working in the back of beyond, but for my uncle Ally this was his local patch! It was a lovely surprise and made me feel quite a home with this new-found family connection with Gairloch.

I stayed on in Gairloch for a few more weeks, but eventually, like Johnny, I had enough of the rural life and returned to Glasgow. Apart from work there was little else for me to do and I missed the companionship of my friends. This early return gave me a few quiet weeks before starting my first year at University.

And on to University

At the end of that summer of '75 I started my Uni course. I was delighted and relieved to have left school, which I had found incredibly sterile and suffocating for the last few years. I felt so free to be unbound by the petty rules of the school and pretty much left to my own devices. I could attend lectures or not, I could do background reading or not, I could go to the Student Union at lunchtime and have a lager and a game of pool. I felt free. My student grant of £30 per week was enough to live a good life, especially as my parents didn't ask for any board and lodging money. Life was opening up for me.

The success of the trip North encouraged me to consider another odyssey, but this time I wanted to go South. I sought adventure and travel away from my home city and country. I wanted to venture outside of Scotland.

I hadn't seen Johnny since the previous summer; however, my brother Gair was up for an adventure. We didn't find work together. While I found work in a small family hotel in Woolacoombe North Devon. Gair got work at Butlin's holiday camp in Bridlington near Skegness.

Going South to the 'Sensuous Land of Beauty'

So I went south to North Devon, where I had found work as a waiter in the Morrell family hotel. The culture of England seemed softer and more sensual than Scotland, especially the far south. I was excited to be heading there for my second odyssey away from home, 1976 proved to be one of the hottest and sunniest summers of the century.

This time I was going on my own, with no friend accompanying me. The date of my departure was to be the evening of Saturday 5th June. I had finished my first-year exams at Uni earlier that week. During the day there was a huge rock festival at Celtic Park with The Who headlining before an audience of 35,000. Gair and I decided we had to go, if I left just before the end, I could catch the last sleeper train South.

What a day. And to go to a rock concert at the Stadium of my football team's arch-rivals. First band I remember were Streetwalkers who had Roger Chapman (ex of Family) as their lead singer, and I really liked his deep gravelly bluesy vocals. 'My Friend the Sun' and 'Burlesque' were highlights. Next up were Little Feat, a funky, laid back Southern Boogie band, with the famous Lowell George on guitar. I had borrowed their albums 'Feats Don't Fail Me Now' and 'Dixie Chicken' from the Students Union record library and loved their mellow sound. A bit out of place in Glasgow's East End, but they really appealed to me. The Sensational Alex Harvey Band were next. Alex was a local Glasgow boy who liked to rock. Brazen and brash the SAHBA didn't have too many frills, but they did like a theatrical, glam rock stageshow. Their show included a huge stage set depicting a wall. And at various times Alex appeared from various parts of the wall rocking away. There was no doubt that The Who were the headliners. They came on around 8pm and went through a set that included 'Baba O'Riley', 'My Generation', 'Pinball Wizard', and of course the revolutionary 'Won't Get Fooled Again'. Pete Townsend electrified us with his windmill guitar playing, and Daltrey passionately screaming 'We won't get fooled again' in his defiant anger. Just before their set ended, I parted from Gair to head off to Central Station for my overnight train. First stop London Euston, then across London to Paddington for the train to Barnstaple.

Glasgow in the 1970s was dark, heavy and violent. I wanted to escape. My plan was to go south to the warmer, softer climes of England. This felt like a big escape. It felt like a bid for freedom. Leaving the heavy industrial city where the soot-stained houses crowding around each other left little breathing space or sunlight. Breaking away from the constrictions of the parental home where the dark gloomy woodwork of the doors and skirting weighed heavily on the soul. Leaving behind the city streets where gang violence erupted easily and frequently. Heading south where adventure and expansiveness lay. Away from the dourness of Calvinism that said if you were happy today then you would pay for it tomorrow. You endured life until it was time to lie in your grave. Heading towards a more open sensual land. This was an important theme in my youth, looking for adventure and travel that would brighten my soul. Bursting through barriers that were restricting and restraining me. Transgressing limits set by parents and society.

I was off to Woolacombe in North Devon. On my own. No older brother. No best friend was going with me. Off to work in a hotel. I was stretching my wings, looking to really live.

I settled in really well with the miscellany of other young men and women working in the hotel. It was the usual mix of students on summer break, hotel staff and those living on the edge of society. Again, the work was not arduous. The summer was hot and dry. There was local life and landscape to explore and enjoy. I was still keenly looking for a lover to dissipate an almost unbearable longing for sex and intimacy. I bought David Bowie records and listened to 'Space Oddity' on the portable record player I purchased on a day trip to Barnstaple, revelling in its vaguely poetic and spiritual 1960's hues.

There was a local surfing scene that attracted a lot of young people. Among the staff were quite a few students. Chestnut haired Rachel had flowing hair down to her shoulders, was beautiful, and was studying English. And there was Rose, a cockney from London, who had worked all her life as a waitress, a down to earth 'girl next door'. There were plenty of women to meet at the discos, and I tried very hard to find someone I could lose my cherry with. I was desperate. My friend Gary had been having sex since he was fifteen, he had even shagged Mary when four of us stayed at my Aunt Maisie's holiday flat in Rothesay. She was the good-looking girl on holiday next door with her family. The closest I had come (sic) was with Hazel McCechnie. We were lying on my sister's bed during my thirteenth birthday party. I managed to dare getting my cock out of my flies, then, not really knowing what to do next I rubbed myself off. I must have made quite a sticky mess of her underwear and tights. Losing my virginity was a major goal, and to be honest I wasn't being very choosy! Apart from that slight blemish in the area of nooky, life was just about as good as it could get.

And Then This Happens…

But that all came crashing in one afternoon after the end of the lunchtime shift. It was another hot day, so we all trooped off to Barricane Beach below the hotel to lie around tanning ourselves and then cooling off in the sea. It was a beautiful sandy beach bordered by low rocky cliffs. Halfway through the afternoon I wanted to go back in the sea to cool down. The only trouble was it was uncomfortably cold, slowly wading out into where the water was deep enough to swim. Unpleasant to feel the cold waters creeping up your legs and abdomen. I decided to dive off one of the tall rocks surrounding the cove. I had done this before and enjoyed the exhilaration of diving through the air before entering the sea and quickly adjusting to the cool water.

I left my friends to slowly wade into the water while I clambered up the rocks. From there I dived about 12 feet into the water. The tide was at low ebb and not too deep. But that wasn't a problem as I knew how to push myself off the bottom when diving into shallow water. I sprung off the rocky ledge, entered the shallow water, pushed off the sandy bottom with my hands, and came to a sudden, dazed stop.

In a concussed haze I tried to stand up and found that my legs wouldn't work. I thought that 'I must've broken my leg.' - they wouldn't push me to standing position. 'Not to worry.' I said to myself, 'Just turn onto your back and wave for help.' Somehow or other I remembered my life-saving training. Rolled over onto my back and floated, lifted my left-arm up to attract attention, just as I had been taught. I hadn't swallowed any seawater, and there was no pain. I was quite in control and wasn't panicking. Comfortably on my back floating. But I was really dazed. Quite quickly a man came over and saw I was in trouble. He called for others to help. Soon a few people were carrying me out of the water. Some of my friends must've gathered and I was taken up the steep curved tarmac path to the hotel. Someone had grabbed me under my armpits, others under my legs. We were soon in the hotel staffroom and I was lain on the table while an ambulance was called.

They seemed to arrive quite quickly. I could make out their dark uniforms and the white band around their caps. They poked me with pins to test for feeling in my legs. Mostly I couldn't feel anything. I was taken out to the ambulance and driven to the Barnstaple A&E. I was flitting in and out of consciousness all this while. There was still no pain. Everything was just an almighty blur. At the hospital I was seen by a young doctor. I really wasn't quite with it as I lay there, not really knowing what had happened or what was happening. This young doctor mentioned that they needed to get my swimming shorts off, and that the best way to do it that would be to cut them off. These were a brand-new pair of black Umbro football shorts that I used as trunks. I was very proud of them, and thought that they looked really cool. But nonetheless I assented to them being cut off. I was in no position to know why they needed to be cut off. I could tell that this doctor was sincerely trying to help me and that this was the best thing to do. He then explained that my bladder wasn't draining and that a catheter needed to be inserted to pass the urine and relieve the pressure.

It was around this time that nursing staff asked me for my next of kin details. I was deeply embarrassed at all the fuss I was causing and really didn't want my parents to know about the huge cock-up I had gotten into. My second prolonged period away from home and I had managed to get into a huge mess and was in hospital! Such an embarrassing position to be in. But what else could I do. I reluctantly gave up my parents address and telephone number. 173 Montford Avenue, Kings Park, Glasgow. 0141-649-5458. My bid to flee the parental home seemed to be coming unstuck. The horizons and doorways that had opened up one month earlier were now closing with a heavy clunking sound. My bid for escape, and freedom from the constraints I had felt in life, was faltering. I would be returning shamefaced and deeply disappointed at my inability to make my way in the world.

The A&E staff thought it best for me to be in a much better-equipped hospital than the small Barnstaple one and I was soon back in an ambulance being transferred to Exeter.

INTENSIVE CARE UNIT

Over the next few days I drifted in and out of consciousness lying in bed in the intensive care ward. By now I had pain in my wrists and chest. But mostly I was unconscious and in a very pleasant, delightful dreamlike cloudy space. I was very contented to be in this once-removed space where I didn't need to do anything. All was peaceful and bright, like some angel drifting on a cloud. This idyll was broken after a few days when I got a strong sense that I needed to return to the world. Deeply disappointed, I gradually left this pleasing, dreamlike space and came back to this world. Back to a bed in a small, quiet hospital room of my own.

I began to receive a few visitors, friends from the hotel where I had been working. They left cards and small gifts and my friend Rose left me a little book of rather sentimental well-meant lines wishing for recovery. Over the days that followed when I was awake, I would pick up that tiny book. Maybe it was only three square inches, and I would do my best to focus on the simple words written there in short sentences. I would struggle to focus and read. Sometimes only managing a line or two, before slipping back into unconsciousness. But I knew I had to return and stay at this task. It was very hard to focus. I could not maintain my concentration for very long. After doing my best, and this sometimes might only be a minute at most, I would be exhausted. And when I relaxed my effort to read I would slip back into unconsciousness totally drained.

As a few days passed I was improving, and emerging more out of my dazed, concussed state. Then I was moved into the main ward. After a few more days my mother and elder sister Fiona arrived from Glasgow. They had taken time off work, come down to Exeter to be by my side and support my recuperation. I still had the pain in my wrists and chest. Doctors came around and tested me for feeling, sensation and movement in my legs. But there was none. I was informed gently and straightforwardly that I would never walk again as I had broken my back. I'm not sure I really believed that. I prayed that maybe I would just lose some power in my legs and be able to walk with calipers. I fantasied that it might make me more attractive to young women, with sympathy for a young disabled boy, but not too disabled. I hadn't forgotten my desire to get my end away.

Fiona and mum were staying in a nearby bed-and-breakfast and coming in every day for the afternoon and evening visiting hours. There were also visits from the hospital Church of England Chaplain. He was much cheerier and affable than the Church of Scotland ministers I knew in my local Kings Park parish church where I had gone for Sunday school. Although he was happier and more pleasing than those Protestant ministers, I didn't feel he was able to really meet me in my predicament. His positivity could only go so far. Fiona and mum were good company and I felt in good spirits. The weather was still hot and sunny and each afternoon, those of us who were not getting up, were wheeled in our beds out onto the ward veranda. There we could enjoy the afternoon sunshine. And also have a short break from the indoors. The attitudes to alcohol seemed very relaxed and I was offered bottles of stout or lager, much to my surprise. Much as I fancied sampling the local beers I declined as I didn't fancy having wind while lying on my back and having a painful chest. The doctors told me the pain in my chest was because I had broken my sternum. There was no explanation for the pain in my wrists. I presumed that I had hurt them while pushing off of the bottom after diving in. Or maybe it was from tightly, unconsciously holding them in the same position close to my chest.

The days went on and there was still no sense of my spinal-cord recovering from the shock of the accident and no movement returning to my legs. I was told that my spinal cord had gone into shock with the trauma from the accident. It could take six weeks for the shock in the spinal cord to relieve itself. This left me in tenterhooks lying in bed waiting to find out if any sensation or movement would return. I continued to be catheterised to drain my bladder. Once a day a nurse would come and connect a saline drip to the catheter valve and my bladder would be filled with the solution. I would have to push the saline back up the tube into the bag: this was all part of my bladder training. I wasn't told what it was training my bladder to do! But it did give me something to do while lying there in that bed all day long. I managed somehow or other to force the saline back up to the bag, but I couldn't tell you how I was doing this, as I did not have any feeling or control of my bladder. Somehow through imagining it, I could send the saline back up to the drainage bag.

Dad arrives!

After a week or so in the Exeter I had a great shock. On that second Saturday morning in hospital, I turned my head to the left and saw my father striding down the middle of the ward. "He must care for me!" were the words that went through my head. Here he was, hundreds of miles from home; he must've taken some time off work and come down by train. I was stunned. I honestly hadn't known that he cared for me. No intimacy, or care, ever seemed to pass between us. Yet here he was. His presence said a lot to me, I was surprised. I always knew that my mother loved and cared for me. No tender words of love passed between us, no hugs or embraces happened between us. I just knew it. And I also felt close enough to Fiona to know there was fondness there. I knew that my mum and sister cared and loved me, and I felt care and love back. We felt very close as a family - my mum, sister and three brothers. But here was my dad. And he must care for me too – otherwise why come all this way?

Dad stayed for the weekend then returned to Glasgow to get back to work. He had come down to see me in hospital. There were no harsh critical words from him. Indeed there were never any words of recrimination from any of my family. I felt foolish, like I had made a huge blunder. I had dared to make a bid for a different, more expansive life and it had come to this. Instead of those horizons opening, it felt like my world was closing in on me, constricting me once again.

Another Existential crisis!

After a fortnight in the Exeter hospital I was to fly up to Glasgow to a spinal injuries unit at Phillips Hill Hospital, South East of Glasgow near East Kilbride. I would be sedated then taken to the local airport where a Piper aircraft that was fitted out for such missions would fly me to Abbotsinch Airport near Glasgow. There I would be met by Ward Staff from the local Spinal Unit and transferred by ambulance. The plane was small, and should only have accommodated myself, but special dispensation was given to allow Fiona to fly with me in the small cramped space.

In those first six weeks I was in continual bedrest. Lying in a 'Stryker' bed with a regular two-hourly interruption to be turned, in order to avoid pressure sores developing. A 'Stryker' bed is a device that has one frame that allows the patient to lie on their back, with another frame that can be placed on top to secure the patient in a kind of sandwich. The whole device can then be turned over and the top frame removed. This means that the patient can be turned over easily and safely by the device. Turning the patient manually could result in possible damage to the spinal cord as the patient isn't so secure. This bedrest gave me plenty of time to think. Reflecting on what had happened was quite devastating in a particular way. Some closely held views about life were slowly shattered. I had never done anything particularly bad or wrong, yet here somehow or other this awful thing had happened to me. I had believed that if you kept your nose clean, didn't do anything particularly bad or wrong, then nothing particularly bad would happen to you. God would look after you. Life would be fair to you, if you were fair to it. Yet here I was lying in hospital with a spinal injury, a broken back, with no sensation or movement in my body below mid chest. This shouldn't have happened. I had done nothing to deserve this awful situation. My dreams had ended. As I reflected on my situation, it seemed that I had played my part, yet God hadn't. This led me to more questioning and so, gradually, my belief in God slowly dismantled. 'How could he exist and let this happen?', became 'He doesn't exist because this has happened.' This seems so simple, yet here was a fundamental value that I had built my life on dissolving like castles made of sand with an incoming tide.

None of the Christian chaplains who visited me in that bed had anything to put my trauma in perspective, they couldn't meet me in my extreme situation. They had no solace for me. Lying in a hospital bed you are freely available to whoever wants to show up and offer you their message. And so I received visits from various chaplains who could offer me nothing. And then there were Sunday services at the bottom of the ward, including the cheery choir singing the Lord's hymns. It all meant less than nothing to me. In fact, it was offensive to have to listen to such stuff. It seemed hollow and meaningless. Yet it was expected to offer some comfort and hope. Well-meant people coming in to offer their best, yet it appeared shallow and false, and really hypocritical me. Meaningless. Sometimes, in this dark and unreachable place, I contemplated suicide. But I had been reading about Eastern religions and their ideas about rebirth. So if there was such a thing as karma and rebirth then in the next life I would have to face what I couldn't face in this life. So suicide was a bit risky. I would need to just get on with my life as it had become. But where was the meaning now? What was life about?

Some of the nursing staff were able to get through to me and help with my rehabilitation. But not all. After six weeks bed rest I was to get up and get dressed. Once you were up and were able to get around in a wheelchair you started rehab. Learning how to use a wheelchair and accomplish daily activities without use of your legs. There was three months of learning new tasks and getting one's strength back. I was allocated the head physiotherapist, a Maltese man who had worked for many years in the Spinal Unit. He had a very good reputation with many patients for getting those in rehab to pull their socks up and make the most of their time in the Unit before discharge. On the morning when he showed up, I was sat up and preparing to get my socks on. He barked a command at me and I immediately barked back. I wasn't going to be bullied by anyone, even if they thought it was for my own good. He obviously sensed my strength of mind, turned around and immediately walked away. I was then allocated another physio who was much more straightforward for me to work with, and who would calmly tell me what I needed to do. I got on fine with the new physio.

Because my belief in God had dissolved, I was now looking for the meaning to life, and explored different religions through reading about them. Mostly I wasn't too impressed by their ideas. After reading an introduction to Hinduism, in my youthful arrogance I wrote it off as being like Christianity but without the guilt around sex: it didn't seem substantially different. I was likewise none too impressed with Judaism after some reading. Somehow or other I came across a title by Christmas Humphreys 'Teach yourself Buddhism'. I found it interesting. Some way through the book Humphreys began to introduce the idea of sunyata. I realised that I had never come across anything like this before. This was something from a completely different source. Here was something I knew nothing about. Here was something I could learn. I was very struck by this teaching. I already had a very favourable impression of Buddhism. I had watched with keen interest the television series 'Kung Fu' with David Carradine. I had been to see the newly released Bruce Lee films. I had heard of Jack Kerouac and the Dharma Bums. But this was my first direct exposure to Buddhist teachings and I was very struck by this new idea. And I wanted to hear more.

However, religion was still tied up with a sense of propriety for me, of being a good boy and doing the right thing. The wilder energies of my being, the sense of adventure and excitement in life as well as the interest in meditative states of mind would somehow need to be accommodated. The hippy ethos was one of 'peace and love', and while I fully subscribed to that, there was much more to me than that motto presented. Yes, I wanted to chill out. Yes, I wanted love. I also wanted to live life fully and change the world. There was a lot of frustration and anger in my newly disabled life, partly due to the great difficulties I faced and the way I found people responding to me now that I used a wheelchair. I hadn't changed, but the response I got from people was changed. Often treated like a child or like a sub-human or like a bad smell. This was a lot to cope with, and much as I was struggling to cope with my disability, society seem to be finding it even harder.

Finding the Dharma in Glasgow – The jewel in the dung-heap!

My eyes were magnetised by the red green and gold colours of the poster every day as I passed on my way to Uni. These colours were swollen with significance for me. They were the Jamaican Rasta colours, and carried with them the sense of soul, rhythm and political change present in the reggae music of Bob Marley and The Wailers, songster poets from Kingston, Jamaica. They sang about their heartfelt longing for Freedom and about Love. It was a long way from Kingston Jamaica in the sunny Caribbean, to Glasgow on the West coast of Scotland, but the longing was the same. The longing for release from any sense of limitation and oppression, the search for an ecstatic joyfulness. I loved the appealing rhythm of these songs, impelling my body to dance.

The colours red green and gold drew my interest to a meditation poster flyposted on a wall by the Victoria Infirmary. Each day as I drove to Uni I passed this way. Each day the poster stood out from the wall, calling to me. Ever since I could remember there was this draw to Meditation. I couldn't tell you why these two contrary elements of music and meditation seemed connected, but they were to me. Whether it was something recalled from the mystery of David Carradine the wandering monk in the television series Kung Fu, seeming similar to the mystical resonance I had felt listening to certain music on the radio in the 1960s. I was about 10 years old, too young to really be part of the hippie era. But getting dressed in the cold Glasgow mornings, listening to songs on the new radio, I intuited significance to some of them. They resonated with a power. I felt that they spoke of something other. Something expansive, adventurous, fresh.

The poster was speaking to me in this language. In post-industrial Glasgow the exotic was emerging. It must have taken a few weeks to mention it to anyone. Then I spoke to Gair, my elder brother. Named after my father, Gair was not unusual in the village of Muir of Ord, near Inverness, where my Dad grew up. And it turned out that Gair had seen the poster as well. We talked excitedly about going along. The poster mentioned a West End address. We had grown up in the southside and had gone to school in the city centre. We were now becoming familiar with the Byres Road, Great Western Road area in the West End as Gair was studying English at Glasgow University. We were often at the Student Union there at the weekend so we had already begun to know the area mentioned on the poster.

My elder brother Gair was bright and precocious in his teens. He had a clear and perceptive mind that took him into areas few of his friends could follow. He had gotten interested in the philosophy of Aleister Crowley and read some of his books. Crowley scared the living bejesus out of me – "Do what you wilt" was Crowley's Law. Gair also had a love of the most avant-garde music of the time; music that was groundbreaking and music that sought to change the world. He wrote about Led Zeppelin's Stairway to Heaven in his English Higher exam. This was a radical departure from the hallowed established tradition of Dickens and Shakespeare that we learned about at Glasgow High School. For Gair, Led Zeppelin's music was art in contemporary terms. And he wrote well enough about Stairway to Heaven in his Higher Exam, that he passed with full colours. He also loved the counterculture, psychedelic folk of the Incredible String Band. To me it sounded dissonant and strange, and only years later did I grow to love them. Gair was tall and solidly built. He stood out with his head of ginger hair. He gathered around him a circle of friends, that he would take with him into his adult years, lived abroad in Germany.

For some reason he phoned our cousin Tom, and mentioned that we were going to a meditation class. Only to be told by Tom that we'd missed it! Tom had gone the previous week for the start of the course. Gair heard that it had been really busy in the flat where it was held. And it had been really good. But we had missed the start, and the course was full. There was a taped lecture series starting the next week though. Tom advised us that we could go to that. It seemed like second best, but we could go. He passed this news on to me, and we made plans for the three of us to meet there the next week.

We met at the appointed time at the agreed location. Gair and I drove over to the West End address in my blue Ford Escort Mark 1 estate car. We parked just around the corner, and it was easy for me to roll down the hill to the 'close' entrance. "Roll downhill" - yes, literally. When I was 18 I had a serious accident, diving into the sea. I injured my back and severely damaged my spinal cord so that I became paralyzed from the mid-chest down. This had happened in early August 1976, a couple of years previously.

In a funny way the accident hadn't really changed my life, it only made it much more intense! Throughout my life I had what you could call mystical experiences: dreams of the future and out of body experiences to mention a few. So in my teens, as well as the ubiquitous youthful desire to change an unjust world, I really wanted to know what life was about. Sure, I learned stuff from parents, teachers, and elders: but none of them seemed to really know about life. They gave out rules that they didn't live up to, bumbled along, maybe got married, have kids, got dull, and died – all after a gradual petering out of life. But what was it all about?

What did it mean? These were ongoing, pressing, existential issues for me during my teens. I was learning loads at school and then at Uni. But never meeting anyone who really knew.

Breaking my back had intensified this painful confusion, unbearably so. My belief in God had dissolved. I had kept my nose clean, never done anything hugely wrong. Yet had ended up paralysed! How could God exist in light of this, that wasn't fair by a long shot! I read around a bit, exploring other religions. Judaism seemed like the vengeful god of the Old Testament and so didn't stand a chance. Hinduism still seemed to have a god, but was much more sensual, and had none of the dark heavy guilt of Christianity. To me it was like Christianity with sex! But still centering around god. Unacceptably similar. Not seeming so much different from Christianity I wrote Hinduism out of the picture - the arrogance of youth.

Then I read an introductory book on Buddhism by Christmas Humphreys. It all seemed ok, even interesting. Then I got to Sunyata, one of the core teachings of Buddhism. I didn't understand this teaching, and because I did not understand, or even comprehend where it was coming from, I knew there was something to learn here. I was intrigued. I was interested and wanted to learn more. All this had led up to me rolling downhill to 13 Kelvinside Terrace South.

OUR FIRST NIGHT

We met Tom at the foot of the stairs. Gair went up the three flights of stairs to the Buddhist Centre just to check it would be ok to go up. He came back down in a few minutes "Yes, it's fine." So up we went. Gair pulling me up, in my wheelchair, the three flights of stairs to the top floor. Double storm doors on the right led into the Glasgow Buddhist Centre. In those days the Centre was a top floor flat in an Edwardian Terrace in Glasgow's West End. That first evening we entered through the front door into a long corridor with a lounge at the far end. The lounge was large and spacious. It was furnished with various odds and sods of dusty old sofas and armchairs that appeared to have been won from a variety of jumble sales. There was a large fireplace to the right as you came in, and ahead of you was a broad, panoramic bay window that took in the back of the iconic BBC building, the Botanic Gardens and the river Kelvin stretching away West to Dumbarton and the Tail of the Clyde. You couldn't help noticing that the flat was brightly decorated in a striking combination of maroon, yellow and blue.

I recall sitting and meditating in front of a beautiful Burmese Buddha image, that was placed in front of a mural of a Tibetan landscape. We didn't receive any meditation instruction. I sat rather uncomfortably on some cushions in the floor. All that I knew about meditation was that it could blow your mind like some powerful drug, that it could be a path to the ecstatic. So I sat there for 20 minutes or so seeking ecstasy.

Listening to Sangharakshita give a talk

Then there was the tea break. After the tea break someone prepared a cassette recorder to play the lecture that was going to be the content of the second half of the evening. They placed the cassette recorder on a small, low wooden table. It was a lecture from someone called Sangharakshita. It was compelling, fascinating, and informative. Part of a series of eight lectures entitled 'The Higher Evolution of Man'. The meditation may not have blown me away but the lecture did. Here was someone who seemed to talk from a deep spiritual experience. Finally! He spoke clearly about Buddhist metaphysics, and I felt he had experienced the depths he was talking about, and he translated it all into modern contemporary ideas. Stunning!

In these talks Sangharakshita explored the idea that life was about Evolution. History had seen the human species evolve through different stages of biological and psychological development – a lower evolution. This lower evolution had been as a species and now the task for humanity was for individuals to evolve – this was what he called the higher evolution. This higher evolution was a combination of religion, mysticism, altruism, psychology and art! A path of increasing self-awareness that used western terms and concepts to convey the traditional Buddhist Path.

We returned every Wednesday following for the whole eight-week course. At the end of the second evening we were in the hall on our way out, when Vairocana (one of the Order Members leading the class) curiously asked us if anybody had introduced the meditation to us. There hadn't been any introduction up till then so we said "No". In the first half of the two evenings, I had just sat there, 'meditating', looking for ecstasy. So we stayed on a bit and Vairocana introduced us to the four stages of the mindfulness of breathing. This was my first real introduction to the art of meditation.

Vibrancy and Energy

There was an incredibly vibrant atmosphere to the Buddhist centre. It was on the third floor of the building. I recall Gair and I pausing on our way out on the ground floor, feeling that vibrancy, that energy coming from the centre, two floors above us. It was so alive. The Order Members who ran the classes were a breath of fresh air, so exuberant and full of life, and they talked to me as an individual, as a person in my own right. This was so invigorating and pleasing after years of being treated like a kid, or subhuman because of my disability, because I used a wheelchair.

My friend Andrew becomes Susiddhi

In October '78, just a few months after me first coming along, Andrew went off on retreat. He came back as Susiddhi. This had been his ordination retreat. He had joined the Order along with a man from Dundee whom I had not met yet. Andrew had been at most of the classes I had gone to and we connected easily. He had recently moved through to Glasgow from Edinburgh. Andrew was quieter than the other order members and maybe this was one of the reasons I connected so easily with him. He was very enthusiastic and had left his job as a pharmacist in the National Health Service to follow his Buddhist life more thoroughly and deeply. Through his job he had been able to buy himself a first floor flat in Bruntsfield Gardens which was in one of the nicer parts of Edinburgh. He had been living there with Uttara for a while. They had run FWBO activities in the flat for a year or so, but without any great success. However, Edinburgh's loss had been my gain as he was becoming a good friend. I really appreciated his ability to be self-possessed while others around him were caught up in emotion. No doubt his time managing a pharmacy department had taught him a few things. He had had a professional career, had lived and travelled abroad. But all this had not really been particularly fulfilling. There had to be something more!

So he had left Bruntsfield Gardens for Heruka, the Glasgow mens' community in Kelvinside Terrace South. He had left a comfortable career, and his spacious flat in one of the nicest parts of Edinburgh, to share a small single room with Ajita in Glasgow in the summer of 1978. The single room they shared in Heruka was not really big enough for two beds. The arrangement was that Ajita would have the single bed, and each evening Susiddhi would bring out a thin camping mat and a sleeping bag from underneath the bed and, using these as his bedding, snuggle down on the floor. Just as well there was something of Scottish simplicity to him that he could thole these sleeping arrangements. Susiddhi had a great respect for Ajita and no doubt this also helped.

Sharing a room with someone offers many moments of close connection. Sharing the simple necessities of life with another forms deep bonds as you get to know the other person not just in how they present to the world but also in their unguarded moments. And so the friendship between the gregarious, one-time Glaswegian gang leader and the quiet, studious, boy who grew up above a pub in a rough coal mining village in Fife, developed.

It was no doubt his deepening friendships in the community was one of the conditions that had helped Andrew deepen into becoming Susiddhi. Being around such a rambunctious lot was bringing Susiddhi out of his shell. For me it was lovely to see the man I was developing a connection with growing more confident. His ordination really brought out more energy, delight, and fun in Susiddhi. He was still the same person after his ordination, in a way even more the character that he truly was. And I now had a friend who I had seen take that momentous step of becoming an order member.

There had been another Scot ordained on that same retreat as Susiddhi. Findlay from Dundee, had been ordained as Suvajra. I had only heard of him in people's conversations as he still lived in

Dundee. Shortly after ordination he would move to Manchester. On one occasion he had found himself in Edinburgh, not far from the community in Bruntsfield. He phoned up to arrange to pop round and was invited over. In high spirits the guys had thought they would share a laugh with him. The front door was open when he arrived. He rang the bell and heard a shout that he should come in, they were waiting for him in the kitchen. Findlay walked along the hallway to the kitchen. Getting into the kitchen he saw Andrew, Ajita, Uttara and Danavira sitting round the table with their trousers around their ankles; broad grins on their faces. Everyone including Findlay had a good laugh at this escapade. Communication was open and nothing held back in their laughter.

The wider FWBO world – another new beginning, and an ending

A month or so after going along to the centre there was a lot of talk between regulars about a new Buddhist Centre that was opening in Bethnal Green in the East End of London. It seemed like a big deal, a huge project that had attracted and needed some of the Glaswegian Buddhists to move there to help. There was something about the way people were talking about the project that spoke of its significance.

Up until now FWBO centres had rented buildings, sometimes squatted in derelict properties, or used a couple of rooms in its communities to hold activities. Fed up with being at the diktat of landlords the community in London had bought a derelict fire station in Bethnal Green – not at all a trendy or alternative part of London's East End. The vision was to transform it into a purpose-built Buddhist Centre. The original plan estimated it would take eighteen months. The young men and women who took this dream project on, soon realized that it was going to be a massive stretch in inconceivable ways to realise the dream. Money was short. Most people were unskilled in building and renovating. The building team moved in to what was really a derelict building, worse than the squats they were used to. It was cold in winter, basic in summer. The shared vision for the place created a very special atmosphere and Idealism soared. This was to be a place that would change the world and the lives of those who got involved in it. Buddhism was coming West and landing in London.

The Hippy idealism of the 1960's carried over into the 1970's and FWBO drew many young people who were looking for a radically new way of life that would transform themselves and their world. Many of that generation looked to the East for a wisdom that was unavailable to them in the West. The FWBO did not draw on wealthy Eastern Buddhists for its funding, everything it did was self-funded and created. To move forward needed the dynamism, ingenuity and creativity of those involved.

The derelict building was now gone. The dream had been fulfilled. The months and years of challenge and hard work had transformed the old fire station beyond recognition. Only the exterior was familiar. Inside was something new. A Western Buddhist Centre had magically risen from the ashes of a fire station. And the opening day was approaching.

A Buddhist Centre in Bethnal Green

Ajita, an Order Member who had just come back off a long 6-month solitary retreat, was encouraging everyone to go down for the December opening of the new centre. Tom was working and so couldn't go. But Gair and I fancied the trip. To be honest it was going to be interesting just going to London, never mind being at the new London Buddhist Centre opening. I think that we must have travelled down on the Thursday because I recall being around the new Buddhist centre early on the Friday and being in the shrine room as a couple of artists winched the new Buddha figure up from the basement.

Another striking thing about this weekend is that I must already have made some connections with the Glasgow Sangha, Sangha being a Buddhist word for spiritual community. Gair and I opted to travel down with Susiddhi in his little blue sports car. Others in the troop who went from Glasgow included Brian (a talented mountaineer and black belt karate man) two art students called Tom and Jerry, and Danavira. My accommodation was on the first floor of 119 Roman Road where I slept on a foam mattress. There was no accessible toilet there or at the Buddhist Centre so I used the public toilets a few hundred yards along Roman Road near the Tube Station.

There was a real buzz around the opening of the Centre. We were told that Sangharakshita would be present and we should be respectful to him. Sangharakshita had founded the Friends of the Western Buddhist Order in 1967 after spending nearly twenty years in India living as a Buddhist and meeting many great teachers there. He was clearly the spiritual head of this movement, and it was his taped lectures we had been listening to on the Buddhism courses back in Glasgow.

Meeting Sangharakshita

In one of the side rooms of the new Buddhist Centre there was an exhibition of paintings depicting various Buddha and bodhisattva figures. It was while I was in this small exhibition space that Ajita introduced me to Sangharakshita, or Bhante as Ajita called him. Bhante is a polite way of addressing a Buddhist Monk. I noticed a man in a tweed jacket, of medium height, with dark hair and broad framed glasses. We spoke a little about the various images and about the differences between Manjusri and Manjugosha. They are both archetypes of Wisdom. Manjusri has a flaming sword poised in his right hand held aloft and holds the book of wisdom to his heart, while Manjughosa has the book of Wisdom placed on a lotus by his side. This was Bhante, the teacher, the founder of FWBO, who I had met. But he appeared to me as being very ordinary, exceptionally ordinary. There was no grand epiphany or drama on meeting him. He was just very present, engaging and normal. I was a bit disappointed at this; it was so in contrast with how impressed I had been with his talks. I must have been hoping for something more dramatic.

Another of our group did have a more dramatic first meeting with Sangharakshita. There was going to be a public talk on the Saturday night and some leaflets had been printed to promote the talk. Volunteers were wanted to hand out the leaflets in London's West End. Brian and some others volunteered. They all went up town, each with a bundle of leaflets, and began to hand them out. Before too long they began to enjoy meeting the people in the busy streets and handing them the leaflets about the big event. Youthful enthusiasm soon took over and there were now approaching the city strollers with confidence. Leaping into their path and boldly thrusting the flyers on the London public. I heard that Brian had been taken up in all this enthusiasm. One moment he had leapt in front of his next target, thrust a leaflet towards them, looked up and found Sangharakshita standing in front of him. Of all the streets in London, and of all the people walking

London's pavements that Saturday morning, Brian had chanced upon Sangharakshita.

I hadn't felt too comfortable about going up the West End on the leafletting mission, and had stayed in Bethnal Green with Gair. It felt enough to be here in a strange town with a new bunch of people. And I was still getting used to people's reactions to me as a wheelchair user.

We had gone along to a display of yoga. I hadn't seen yoga before and we watched as around a dozen people were taken through various poses. I had heard about yoga, but had never seen anyone do it. It was so different to any other physical exercise I had seen – nothing like football, rugby or swimming! Somehow or other I felt a bit uncomfortable looking on at the bodies in the various yoga poses. I think the yogis also felt some of this discomfort

'Here we are as some strange kind of exotic freaks, performing exotic acts, for the straights to goggle at.' I overheard one man confiding to his friend.

The Buddhist centre was so full in the afternoon for the official opening ceremony that we were unable to get in to the main shrine room. There was a live transmission broadcast to a screen in the adjacent small shrine room. So Gair and I had to be content with being next door to the main event. We sat in front of the standing Buddha figure watching the transmission from a packed shrine room next door.

On the Sunday evening we went along to Sangharakshita's talk entitled 'Authority and the Individual in the New Society'. The talk was given in a nearby public hall. It was a spacious Victorian building whose grandeur was now a bit faded and of another era. This was the first time that I had heard Sangharakshita speak live. Dressed once more in the tweed jacket and the other clothes I had seen him in the day before, he now stood on stage, addressing his audience. The ordinary appearance was still there. However, there was an energy and conviction in his voice as he mentioned the significance of the day before, exploring with great clarity and creativity the subject of his talk. After about 10 minutes or so, Gair whispered in my ear that he had to go to the toilet. He squeezed along the narrow row of seats to make his exit. I sat on listening attentively to Sangharakshita, absorbed in his talk, and following the unfolding of his ideas. Gair seemed to be taking a long time in the loo. More of the talk unfolded and still no return of my brother. I was really moved, intrigued and stimulated by Sangharakshita's message clearly coming through the talk. Disappointed that I was not sharing this experience, a highlight of the weekend, with my brother. Sangharakshita spoke passionately of a New Society, a society based on Buddhist values, and how this had emerged in the East End of London. I had witnessed the strong connection and sense of purpose of those who were involved in the transformation of that old fire station in Roman Road, converting a derelict fire station into a beautiful space devoted to Buddhist practice.

I had become disgruntled and disillusioned in my youth by a lot of what I'd seen around me. It looked to this 20-year-old youth that there was plenty of jaded hypocrisy, cynicism and lifelessness in the old institutions. During my teens I had wanted to change this world, I had sought to find some really radical people who were truly living, really changing this spent world. Sangharakshita's words and ideas seemed to articulate and formulate for me, a dim sense of something I already knew of what the world could look like and how a new world could be brought into being. There were values here, and a way to practice these values with others who were enthused and alive to these possibilities. This was exciting and seemed to be awakening in me an understanding that all this was really possible.

A PAINFUL PARTING

Gair and I had shared much of these values and longings during our teens. Not only was he my elder brother, in whose footsteps I often followed, he was also my soul brother.

During Sangharakshita's talk I somehow knew that he wasn't happy with it and this disturbed me. That my life might diverge from my soul brother was a big worry. And it proved true. Gair returned about 10 minutes after the end of the talk. It turned out that he felt Sangharakshita was being snobbish when he remarked that the Buddhist Centre was being established in the East End, rather than in one of the more upmarket districts of London such as Westminster or Victoria. I had taken this as a sign of Sangharakshita being pleased that it wasn't just a middle-class thing that was happening, but something with roots in a deep, common humanity. We had both come across plenty of pretentious, conceited attitudes about class in our lives, and were shocked and disillusioned when we came across these attitudes. Our mother had always insisted that we 'were as good as anyone', thus inculcating a strong, competitive Glaswegian egalitarianism in us. And at our fee-paying secondary school and at University we had come across plenty of snobbery.

Gair had reacted to the talk and I instinctively knew this was irreversible. He had decided to leave go for some drinks in a local pub. This deeply concerned and saddened me - to lose my brother's companionship as we explored Buddhism and the FWBO.

We left London later that very night. The journey back was fairly uneventful compared to the richness of the weekend. We did miss our turning from the M1 onto the M6 in the dark so the journey home was longer than it might have been. During this return to Glasgow I felt filled with the richness of the weekend.

Back in Glasgow there were consequences to Gair's response to the talk. The Buddhist classes were on a Wednesday evening. After London, Gair decided he preferred going to midweek football matches rather than continue with our joint exploration of Buddhism. We were both Rangers fans since boyhood, during the lean years, when our rivals Celtic were in the ascendancy. Managed by Jock Stein, Celtic triumphed in Europe and won nine league titles in a row. It wasn't a good time to be a Rangers fan, and coming second best. Our great grandfather, Peter Nimmo, had been one of the founders of Rangers Football Club and we had an almost mythical connection through him to the Gers. This was much to my Highland dad's annoyance, like many he abhorred the club due to the privileged position they held. Gair really enjoyed mingling with the down to earth types he met in this footballing world, and a sense of camaraderie he found there.

So while he went off to Ibrox to watch football, I went to Kelvinside Terrace to pursue the Dharma and my involvement in Friends of the Western Buddhist Order. We talked about his reservations, and I could see that it was a bit of an institution with imperfections. Even so, I felt FWBO offered me the possibility of addressing the deep restrictions I felt, and offered me something of an open horizon that was tinged with freedom and adventure. Maybe my need was greater. And so we parted. Sadly. Our connection remained strong and deep but our paths diverged. Maybe I had more to resolve since breaking my back. Disability and using a wheelchair had intensified the existential angst I had already felt in my teens.

I felt that Buddhist life as presented by Sangharakshita would be one of meaning and meditation, as well as friendship and adventure. And I found this such a compelling combination of much I was looking for in life.

My first retreat

The weekend trip to London had shown me more of what the FWBO had to offer. There was a sense of freedom and adventure about these people as well as a commitment to Buddhist practice. Then there was the spiritual depth of Sangharakshita. The Glasgow Sangha had a particular love and depth of meditation practice. Ajita had just come off a six-month retreat and was going to be leading a two-week meditation retreat over the Christmas and New Year holidays. My friend Susiddhi had told me about the retreat and encouraged me to come. It was to be held in a youth hostel at Rowardennan, at the foot of Ben Lomond, by the shore of Loch Lomond.

'Why don't you just come for the weekend and see how you feel. If it's going well you can stay longer. If you want to, go home after the weekend.' Susiddhi said.

This was enough to get me on the retreat. I hadn't been on a retreat before and was a bit apprehensive. We would be meditating a lot, and listening to lectures. We would be eating vegetarian food. It would be a bit intense. But I was intrigued. I was up for the adventure.

Rowardennan Youth Hostel is around an hour's drive north-west of Glasgow. It lies on the east side of Loch Lomond, the quieter side. The main road north heads up the west side of the loch. The rugged slopes on the east side don't permit passage by car even down by the loch shore. So, although Rowardennan is quite easy to get to, it is quiet and remote. This would be the second winter retreat held there. These winter meditation retreats had taken on epic dimensions. The idea of meditating in the mountains like the Buddhist yogis of the East, captured the imagination of many, and a number of the retreatants would venture north from London and Brighton. We heard tales of the yogis of the mystical land of snows, Tibet. In particular we had begun to hear of Padmasambhava, the Lotus-born Tantric Guru. He had conquered the Demons of Tibet allowing for the Buddhist tradition to be able to flourish in this new land north of India. We heard how Padmasambhava had started the 'old school' of Nyingmapa Buddhism in Tibet. These Nyingmapas were not necessarily monks, some were married. They were wild and unconventional. Not bound by stuffy monasticism. They were living in the mountains, cave dwellers, beyond the trappings of genteel custom. They were authentic. We heard how in the Tibetan spiritual community the wild yogis, the monastics, and the lay people were united by their spiritual practice and ideals. Different lifestyles did not prevent them from coming together with an appreciation of what it really meant to practice Buddhism. These were the people we longed to emulate.

So instead of eating way too much at Christmas, instead of boozing it up over New Year, the Glasgow Sangha went off to the mountains to meditate in deep winter.

I was to drive there in my blue Ford Escort estate on my own. I found my way out to Loch Lomond easily enough. I had been driving since passing my test the year before. The youth hostel is not a grand building, but it was indeed in grand surroundings. The loch was only 100 yards from the front door and had its own jetty. The rear of the building backed onto trees that rose up the slopes, first to Ptarmigan Hill, and then on to the majesty of Ben Lomond. The accommodation was basic. A few dormitories with bunkbeds. Communal toilet and shower block. There was a large open dining space, with a step down to a lounge area. We converted one of the back rooms into a shrine, complete with Buddha image and space to meditate.

We rose at 6:30am and meditated for two hours before a breakfast of thick porridge and toast. Then listened to a talk of Sangharakshita on the symbols of Tantric Buddhism. Afternoons were free to explore the lanes around the hostel, or venture down by the Loch shore, or wander up the mountain. Meditation again before dinner. Meditation and puja in the evening: puja is a buddhist devotional practice of chanting verses, and Mantras invoking the qualities of enlightened beings.

A STILLNESS THAT VIBRATED AND HUMMED

I really enjoyed the stillness of the meditations. The shine room developed an atmosphere of dense peace. A stillness that vibrated and hummed. Through chanting mantra, we evoked archetypal figures who embodied the compassion, energy and wisdom of Enlightenment, and these beings seemed to walk amongst us. I loved being with the other retreatants, who all seemed so alive and interesting. A warm friendliness was created around and between us. It was moving to see the deep friendship formed between people. We developed loving-kindness in our meditation, and that quality poured out into the space between meditations, creating deep bonds between everyone on the retreat. It was great to feel part of this community.

As you can see, I got on very well over the weekend and I can remember Susiddhi approaching me on the Sunday afternoon to ask how I was doing. It must have been pretty apparent that I was having a great time but he asked me anyway. Maybe just to confirm things.

'Yes,' I said 'the weekend retreat has been really great. I think I'll stay for the whole fortnight.'

'I thought so.' he said 'I thought you would enjoy the retreat. Glad you're staying.'

And so, my first retreat turned into a two-week intensive meditation retreat.

A certain curiosity about meditation was one of the prime movers in getting me along to the Buddhist Centre. During the retreat we sat for many hours a day. Of course, some of these meditations were what the Zen tradition would call 'dead sitting'- more of an endurance than a creative unfolding of skilful, expanded states of mind. But I had many meditations where clarity emerged, where I felt centred in my being. Peaceful, blessed states of mind unfolded, when not only was I in this peaceful state of mind but the world itself was peaceful. In other meditations I would experience an incredible tension and if I sat in this tension long enough it would release and tears would roll down my cheeks. I never knew what the tears were about, but it felt good to be letting go.

This release was especially welcome, as there had been so much upheaval in my life since breaking my back. I'd had a lot of change to deal with and there was a fair amount of anger and dark moodiness around for me in those years. Sitting there on the meditation cushion for hours on end I would sometimes find myself in these dark heavy moods. Completely immersed in it.

And then, like the sun emerging from behind clouds, in a moment my mood would lighten and brighten. Somehow or other my mood changed; I couldn't really say how. A different perspective arose and everything would be alright. In one sense everything had changed and in another, nothing had changed at all. As I write these words tonight at my kitchen table it doesn't surprise me that my dark moods lightened. How could they not! We were practising loving-kindness meditation, so how could feelings of love for myself not arise to penetrate and dissolve even the darkest of my moods. Sitting there for hours holding my experience in meditative awareness. It was inevitable that I should resolve difficulties. These days we have a saying - 'feelings just want to be felt.'. In those hours of meditation, I was certainly feeling things. And in holding those feelings in an open loving awareness, the feelings were fully felt. Having delivered their message, the feelings now departed.

A MEDITATION MASTER

Ajita was a master at leading retreats. With an acute sense of the collective atmosphere and a resilient, resourceful, ebullient and indomitable character, he never allowed us to become morose, sitting there for long hours. Spiritual life was an adventure, the heart was to be explored, Life to be lived to the full. He would periodically quote "Rabindranath Tagore "I know I shall love death, because I have loved life.' This was one of his favourite quotes. He himself, seemed able to meditate for long periods filled with happiness and bliss. Why be miserable when you could have the bliss of the Yogi?

These were the possibilities he presented to us as we meditated. It was our choice?

Over the retreat. I became familiar with two mantras. One was the mantra evoking compassion, and as I chanted it a light playful mood would overcome me. The other one evoked Padmasambhava, and a fearless vigour would arise, the feeling of being a spiritual warrior. There was also the mindful walking practice which we did in between periods of sitting meditation. Walking practice would bring much-needed respite to aching hips and knees, while still keeping our minds focussed. At first, I didn't take part in the mindful walking because I couldn't walk. Soon I figured out the principle of mindful walking was *mindful movement*. So whilst I couldn't walk mindfully around the room, I could mindfully push my wheelchair around the room. Once I had figured this out, I joined in the mindful walking.

Although the retreat was intense, I never felt prescribed to limit myself or curb my self-expression. The opposite was true: I felt encouraged to be just who I was, and how I was.

'In this limited self with all our hangups and habits, we can still get Enlightened.' Ajita said, 'There isn't a right type of Buddhist, there are just Buddhists practising, heading for enlightenment.'

At the end of a meditation session you could sit on savouring the experience, sitting with spaciousness, expansiveness or bliss. After one early-morning session Ajita rang the bell to finish the first meditation, the first bell was followed in a few minutes by the bell to stand up. After standing we needed to clear the space to allow us to circumbulate the room clockwise. To go anticlockwise, to go widdershins, was thought to be unlucky. This morning one of the elderly retreatants sat on in his space in the centre of the room. Still shrouded in the darkness of a winter's morning, we carefully placed our meditation cushions and blankets around him, we did not want to disturb his deep meditation. He sat on unmoved. We were impressed at this show of spiritual attainment and maturity. Mindfully we walked for the 10 minute period. We were all very careful not to disturb our spiritual friend's meditation. He sat on immovably. We collected our cushions and blankets at the end of the walking period and got ready to meditate again. We sat in our meditation postures and quietened our body then our mind. In the ensuing silence the heavy breathing and occasional snoring of our friend was unmistakable. He was asleep. We all cracked up with laughter.

In the middle of winter not many visitors passed near the youth hostel. It was possible to go along the narrow roads to the woods of moss-laden silverbirch and not see a solitary soul. The hostel had its own jetty, still in its own grounds, down by the loch 100 yards from the front door. From the wooden jetty you could look across the loch to the Arrochar Alps, rising above the western shore, and sprinkled with snow at this time of year. Looking behind the hostel you could see how the woods came down from the mountains to embrace the back of the building. The shrine room was at the back and its windows looked out into this dense woodland, the presence of the mountain reaching into the man-made world. During these retreat days our exploration of inner landscape was matched by our exploration of the local geography. On New Year's Day some braced the icy waters of the loch and swam out from the jetty. At the end of the retreat a posse of eight of our number climbed up the back over the Ptarmigan Mountain to the peak of Ben Lomond. Mostly these were fit young men, although one climber with only one full leg, and another man with severe spondylitis ankylosis that stooped his upper back into a pronounced hunch. All reached the summit of the Ben, passing through snow fields near the summit. We scaled spiritual ideals and one of Scotland's best-known Munros, a mountain over 3000 feet. The same spirit of adventure, courage and energy taking us up the spiritual heights as took us up the geographical heights.

The Retreat ends, all things change, returning to the world

All things are impermanent and change. Time marches on. The retreat ended. The drive back home took us through the rundown district of Maryhill in Glasgow, where we saw the human debris, leftover from New Year celebrations. Grey ashen faces, slumped bodies, directionless wandering. In contrast we felt bright, alive, with a vision for life. Two weeks in the elemental countryside brought vigour to our bodies. Two weeks on meditation retreat left our souls imbued with truth, meaning, and friendship.

The glow of the winter retreat gradually dissolved into the normality of life. For me a couple of reminders remained. The food on the retreat had been vegetarian and I had felt a lot lighter and healthier. There was also an ethical dimension to my decision, I wanted to cause less harm in the world. So I became vegetarian. I now cooked my own vegetarian meals in the family home. I stopped eating fish and meat. I didn't really have much knowledge about how to eat well from my vegetarian diet, so my diet was nutritionally poor but rich in idealism. I also started to meditate in my bedroom. I'd get down on the floor from my wheelchair, as this was more comfortable, and try do the meditations I had learnt. With a lot of interest and enthusiasm but not much experience of deep meditation. Nothing was said at home about these changes. I just ate vegetarian food and meditated. Whether my parents and brothers were worried or interested I didn't really know. One Sunday afternoon I was meditating in my bedroom when my mum came in with the Hoover to tidy up. Her Sunday's were given over to washing and cleaning. I sat on, down on the floor beside my chest of drawers, with my eyes closed meditating. She carried on with the hoovering, cleaning around me, careful not to bump me with the hoover and disturb me.

University continues

Other things carried on as normal. I continued with the university course at Strathclyde. I was now in the third year of my B.Sc. course. The man who began the course had visited my school during my final year. He had been very passionate about this new course. He had started it just the year before. As a successful businessman he had seen the need for university graduates entering the workplace to be knowledgeable in both the financial and technological side of industry. He hoped to produce a generation of graduates with expertise in both these areas. His enthusiasm had been infectious and I was keen to be studying on a course led by someone who had much knowledge and knew the relevance of what was being taught. In the first year we had studied physics, mathematics and some IT. For the second year we had to specialise in a subject from each of two lists – one Technological and one Business Studies. The business studies list had accountancy and economics. The technology list had mechanical engineering, electrical engineering, and fibre science.

I had chosen accountancy and fibre science. Although I had enjoyed economics at school I went for accountancy because there was a good chance of getting a well-paid job at the end of it. Jobs for accountants were plentiful, and the financial rewards were said to be good; and I knew I was good with numbers. The technological choice was also quite easy. I had visited the mechanical engineering department which was incredibly noisy and very dirty: a black grease seemed smeared everywhere. Electrical engineering was based on extremely complex maths, and we were told that it was a very difficult option, but fine if you were proficient with abstract equations. The fibre science department was rather peculiar. It was here that the textile cone of Concord, Britain's first supersonic jet airplane, had been developed. It was reported to be the easiest option. I was intrigued by this subject. There are all sorts of weaving and knitting machines, as well as chemistry labs, where you learned the makeup of different types of fibre as well as the composition of the dyes that were used to colour them. Being interested in fashion, a sideline of my interest in the pop culture of the 1970s, and being a young Glaswegian male who wanted to dress well to impress the ladies I chose textile technology.

I had enjoyed the fibre science course, it was interesting using the different knitting and weaving machines, as well as dyeing different types of fabrics and seeing how they came out.

Sexuality and Disability meets Calvinism!

My last year in uni coincided with my first year of involvement with FWBO Buddhism. Since breaking my back I had thrown myself headlong into the academic side of the course. I thought that this was something I could do well, and an area that my new physical disability would not restrict me. There were many restrictions and disappointments in other areas of my life. Many of the haunts that I used to frequent did not hold the same appeal and frequently they were pretty inaccessible for a wheelchair user. Dancing, drinking, and women were not the same. I used to really enjoy going to Discos to dance and try and get a lumber. Those first years using a wheelchair I felt much too self-conscious to attempt to dance in public. Wheelchair users were a rare sight in the 1970s and I don't ever remember seeing a 'crip' dancing. That would have been too much to expose oneself to mockery. I got quite a lot of interest from women, but I sensed so much pity in their response and so much mothering , and smothering, that I generally kept my distance. I mostly stayed clear to avoid frustration and disappointment. I was still coming to terms with disabled sexuality. I had no normal sensation from mid chest down, could not get an erection easily, and I definitely could not master the pelvic agility to thrust and penetrate a women. I felt a loss of masculinity. I was going through a tremendous change. I was so confused about who I was. What did it mean for me to be a man?

Even before becoming paraplegic I had struggled with the model for masculinity that 1960s Glasgow offered me as a boy. I had found that model to be hard, controlled, repressive, regressive. In my teens I had followed the gender explorations of David Bowie and the Glam rock of Mark Bollan's T Rex . Feminism was in its early days and rising. My father had his copy of 'The Female Eunuch' by Germaine Greer, although I never really understood the significance of this. The authoritarian patriarchy was being challenged. Men's role was changing rapidly and profoundly.

I was slightly terrified of women, I certainly did not understand them, and knew that there was ways of perception and intelligence beyond me. All through my teens I had been quite moody. A mood would descend on me like a weather pattern coming in off the Atlantic. I had very little sense of what brought them about and how they lifted. Women seemed to live in this world of emotion, have an intelligence of the heart and personal relations that was out of my league. They could know more about what I was feeling than I did myself, and I found myself threatened by being so out of control and like putty in female hands.

I longed painfully for sex, and the union it offered. I could fantasise about what it was like; I wanted the sensations it seemed to be about. And I couldn't relate to women. I was a decent, well-behaved chap; and was confounded by women. They seemed like an unsolvable riddle to me.

I kind of thought that I was no longer able to be sexual because I couldn't be the hard physically dominant, thrusting, aggressive male that my culture told me to be. I knew this was not the whole story, but I did not know the rest of the story. I was certainly confused. It was easier to focus on the certainties of learning than it was to get lost in the confusion of expectations, and false hopes that close relations brought about.

In a mood of classic transcendence, I aspired for the spiritual. I put my lot in with the spiritual over the material, as the material confused and frightened me. I could see friends from school have their lives, getting lost in work, girlfriends and children. Independence was lost to the emotional demands of the relationship; open boundaries became closed; the dreary jobs necessary to pay for offspring denied adventure.

Yet I was still subject to mystical longing. I thought I could have mystical union, delight through meditation and spiritual practice. To some extent the world seemed to be closing its doors to me, worlds I had expected to move into appeared wheelchair inaccessible. The denial of physical access was enough for me to rule out many worldly possibilities. And I pulled these doors shut myself and went off into a Buddhist path looking for fulfilment. My body was crippled but my mind wasn't. I was determined that although my body was disabled my mind would not be.

My career goes down the plughole

As my interest in Buddhism evolved, my interest in following a career evaporated. In the summer of 1978 I had a period of work experience in the offices of Coats Patons , a famous textile multinational company with headquarters in Glasgow city centre. I got this work experience as part of the University course. For a number of weeks, I went in to their prestigious office block in West Regent Street and worked there in an administrative role. The offices were accessible enough for me to enter the building unaided and use the lift to the floor where I worked. There was an accessible toilet. They had cleared a pathway to the desk where I worked, to the photocopier and toilet, for which I was very thankful. I enjoyed being there and working with the many staff. I can recall one Belgian man who had worked in the company for many years. It was unusual to have a Belgian around! He loved his coffee and introduced me to the novel idea of drinking cold coffee.

Getting around the office to talk to other colleagues was limited by the small gaps between the desks and other furniture, it really was not easy. The same was true of other floors in the building. And the older buildings in the company weren't accessed easily: West Regent Street was modern and just about as accessible as you could get – yet still limited. I saw that an interesting job, a career job, would involve travel to other locations. Given that accessible buildings were the exception back then, I couldn't see how a career was a viable option for me as a wheelchair user. It could be that now I was seeing the world through the eyes of a wheelchair user I was seeing more difficulties than solutions, but I couldn't see how I could negotiate spaces that were wheelchair unfriendly. And maybe I closed that door a bit too quickly.

I was also beginning to see some distasteful sides to business. The job in Coats involved reading the Management Accounts of their international affairs and these showed the transfer of funds between divisions and how money was being switched around to minimize tax liability and maximize profits. I saw how activities were transferred to countries to maximize profit without concern for the livelihoods of their employees.

One evening when I was lying in bed during my recuperation at Phillipshill Hospital my Dad came to visit.

'I've got some bad news for you, Ken' he said 'I've been made redundant.'

He was clearly distraught and worried about what this would mean for the family's finances. He was now in his fifties, and had worked loyally for Balfour Beatty on several projects for nearly twenty five years. He had started as a joiner, then become a foreman, and general foreman. Now he had been made redundant for no good reason, and at his age he could not see any future prospects. Big business was not to be trusted!

I was certainly good with numbers, and could easily work financial data to create profit and loss accounts. I was also familiar with management and tax accounts. Early on at University my ability to master these skills gave me a good feeling about myself. I even found that taking complex financial situations and working out end of year accounts and balancing books brought about a euphoric feeling something similar to meditation. One of the meditation practices that I had started practising involved empathising with others and seeing that at heart we are all the same – we all want to be well and happy. In the fifth stage of the metta bhavana meditation you are encouraged to develop a wellwishing for every person on the planet, regardless of gender, race or class. I began to feel for the people affected by Management decisions. Most financial decisions were driven by profitability without any feeling for the people affected. I began to think that this wasn't right. Just to make business decisions solely for financial profit became distasteful to me.

As my time at university unfolded, I began to lose interest in the degree course. It wasn't going to be a base for a career. It wasn't the way to progress my life. I did consider packing it in. Having discussed this with my new friends, that course of action seemed a bit reactionary. In the end I thought it would be much better to finish what I had started. So, I saw the course out and graduated, but much to the disappointment of my course tutors, I did not go on for another year to get an honours degree.

MY INTEREST IN BUDDHISM DEEPENS

My real interest was moving into the Buddhist world. I found myself fascinated by ideas that helped me understand and open life up. Ideas that rang true. I found myself meeting and befriending people from such different walks of life. People, who I thought exciting, Bohemian and interesting.

In my own background we were mostly working class: my father worked on building sites, my mother a part-time office worker. This was the world my family lived in; my uncles and aunts all worked in building or in offices. In these new discussions there was much talk about creativity. This usually meant the creativity of the artistic world of music, literature, or painting. I had felt like a fish out of water in art classes at secondary school. No one in my family seemed very involved in the business of creating music or literature. Living a creative life seemed very attractive and colourful to me. Yet I had no interest in the arts. So, what could I do? I was very taken by the idea of evolution. Seeing that life was an unfolding process. Hearing that one could create one's own self through meditation and a radical lifestyle appealed to me. It reminded me of the lyrics in the Talking Heads song 'Seen and not Seen': 'by keeping an ideal facial structure fixed in his mind....Or somewhere in the back of his mind....That he might, by force of will, cause his face to approach those of his ideal.'

After my accident I had felt a lot of frustration and anger, and was quite unhappy at times. It might be the way I was treated like a kid by some; or frustration at not being able to walk up stairs to get to a party; feelings of separation and alienation because I had to get in buildings by the back door and not the front door like everybody else. Somehow, I felt that I was abnormal because I was unhappy at times, and was suffering. Suffering wasn't cool and I thought my friends would disown me if I admitted to them that I was unhappy. The Buddhist teachings of the four Noble truths brought relief to me. This teaching says that there is suffering in the world, and it is part and parcel of being alive. This was such a relief - I wasn't weird after all.

I was having discussions where people were talking to me. Since I had started to use a wheelchair, I had noticed that people would regularly talk to the person standing beside me; to the person accompanying me. This used to be called the 'Does he take sugar?' mentality, when the question is addressed to the able-bodied person rather than the disabled person. As if the disabled person is unable to speak for themselves. This is incredibly annoying, belittling and humiliating. I'm glad to say that it is much less these days due to increased understanding around disability. I found it so refreshing to be addressed and engaged with as an individual. I can still recall the thrill of being seen and recognized when Danavira asked me my views about something the group was discussing. He was interested in me. I was so grateful and relieved for that.

Those early Sangha members

The Glasgow Buddhist community in those days was a mixture of some who had been around in the very early days, when it was an unaffiliated Buddhist group, to the more recent arrivals. Some came in jeans and T-shirts. Some came in tweed jackets. There were different generations of members, some who had been attracted during the Beat Generation of the 50's, and those who connected during the Hippie Generation of the 60s and 70's.

I was very fond of many of them. We had one old Glasgow gent, small, bald and slightly rotund. A very gentle man who was attracted to Buddhist ideas of Freedom and renunciation - yet still lived at home with his mother.

Occasionally a man with a slight Western Isles accent would grace the evenings. Solid in his being, dark hair, rosy cheeks, with a lilt in his voice. Quiet. Reputed to write plays for BBC Radio Scotland. The creative arts were not really present in my family background, yet here was somebody who lived as a playwright and wrote plays for the radio! This was completely out of my known world and so Menzies Mckillop intrigued me. I never knew anything personal about him. BBC Scotland had validated him as a writer. For me his presence at the Buddhist Centre gave it some kind of validation.

Another true gentleman worked on boats in harbours around the west coast of Scotland. He could only come when his work on the boats' radar permitted. A Scottish engineer. Precise. Clear. Without the cold heart often associated with those qualities. Bill seemed to have great integrity and a calmness about him.

I loved rubbing shoulders with these older men who came along. We talked. They were enthusiastic without getting carried away by the excesses of youth. They had lived some life, had gravitas and experience. My own father was usually too tired out after work to talk with us. A quiet Highlander. He was a bit of a mystery. An absent father who worked six or seven days a week. Out at six thirty in the morning before I got up, and back after six in the evening, sometimes after we had already finished dinner. I never really knew him, never really knew his world, he never told us of it. He had a fiery temper that blazed and receded quickly, without warning. I and so was wary of him. These older men took me seriously, we discussed issues, explored life. In my rather timid and restrained being I was intrigued and never shocked by these wise gentlemen. I loved them. They were safe!

And the Order Members - bright free and dynamic!

I was shocked, deeply shocked and excited by many of the younger sangha members. Anarchists. Musicians. Scientists. Those who took drugs to expand their minds. Young men with beautiful girlfriends. Those who had hitchhiked all over Europe. Wow, these guys were living free!

The classes at the Buddhist Centre were being run by guys in their 20s or early 30s. I was astonished that they had come to be leading a Buddhist Centre at what seemed like a young age. I was also relieved in a way, because it meant that I could relate to them easily as age didn't get in the way. They seemed just a bit further along the path than I.

Danavira had studied English at Strathclyde University and was one of the core order members. He seemed to be at all the classes

I went to. He was dynamic, ebullient, and voluble. He was stockily built, with dark hair and about 5'9" tall. His communication was direct and friendly. He had grown up in the east end of Glasgow. He talked about the days when they had lived in a Gray Street basement flat and meditated many hours of the day. So intensely had they explored one Buddhist meditation on death that when they walked down the city streets they saw people as skeletons. Danavira had a great sense of humour. He was moving way beyond his working class East End roots that weren't enough for him. I heard that he was training to be a bus driver and a bit of me relaxed. He was so obviously practising Buddhism at a depth beyond me. A lot of Buddhism seemed very exotic and far removed. I could relate to him being a bus driver, a lot of my friends were now working as joiners, printers or in offices. My father was a foreman on building sites, my mother worked in an office. This said that I too, could be a Buddhist. I was relieved that Buddhism could span both the exotic and the known.

It was Vairocana who had first taught me to meditate. He was quieter than the others. He didn't say a lot, but when he did, it was very clear and interesting. He was another Glaswegian, also working class, from one of the western suburbs of the city. He had a twin brother, Charlie, who appeared from time to time but Charlie wasn't interested in Buddhism.

Then there was Dhammarati, he also was around a lot in my early days. He had a very clear understanding of Buddhism. He talked about a spiritual search that had taken him first of all to Christianity in his hometown of Larkhall, a small town 20 miles east of Glasgow, renowned for its strong adherence to the Orange Lodge. There was some deep sensitivity resident in him that had carried him forward on a spiritual search until he had come across

Sangharakshita, FWBO and the spiritual depth he found there. He had worked as a psychiatric nurse for a period. There was a finesse and grace about Dhammarati that clearly wasn't of Larkhall. When I saw him walk, it struck me as being particularly graceful and swaying, as if he was enjoying every little movement. He had a beautiful long-haired girlfriend who was at Art School, and he himself was really interested in art, radical anarchism and socialist ideas.

And of course there was Ajita. He had been on a six month solitary during the first weeks of my involvement. I soon got to know him. Like Danavira he was ebullient, dynamic and very friendly. He had grown up in Spittal a rough working-class estate not far from Kings Park where I had grown up. Ajita was maybe around 5'8" and stocky, indomitable, with a shock of blonde hair, square jaw and large bold face and physique. He had been a leader of the local gang. Gone through psychedelia and arrived at the Dharma. He was a very astute guy in many ways, he read people really acutely, was very friendly and had a passion for open authentic communication. His intelligence was not intellectual yet he had a more than impressive commonsense and deep spiritual perceptiveness. He wouldn't be fooled by appearances. And I really have to mention his great love of meditation and ritual. In many ways he was the real deal. His depth of meditation practice was delightful and not forced. There was a radiance about him that stemmed from the absorbed places he experienced whilst sitting in meditation. And he was fearless and determined.

Uttara had been the hard man in the same gang as Ajita. They had grown up together in the Spittal district. Their paths had led them both from Glasgow ganglands to Buddhist practitioners. Uttara was taller than Ajita, he was closer to 6 foot. He had a strong, wiry physique. Dark curly hair, coal black eyes, and a penetrating gaze that gave you no hiding place. Yet there was a profound tenderness that accompanied the fierce gaze, and on many occasions I felt gently held by him when I felt exposed or ill at ease.

Guhyananda was also around. He was much softer and quieter than the Glasgow order members. Originating from the north, he had an airy quality to him, a lightness of touch and always a twinkle in his eye.

This was the array of order members around in my early days of involvement. At that point there was a common interest amongst them in the punk movement, perhaps a shared interest in breaking through the superficial to authentic communication. And a shared interest in energy that was bright, free and dynamic. There was nothing staid about FWBO Glasgow.

Open Communication

In this atmosphere I felt I had to be totally honest and open in my communication. If I wasn't, then the response would be that I was blocking the energy of the other person. If truth be known, I was emotionally blocked in many ways then. I didn't really know what I felt, and was apprehensive around sex and communicating directly and openly from my heart. I had been brought up to be polite and respectful and there was little heart to heart talking that I remember in my family. My parents had their important conversations in the privacy of their bedroom. Their whispered disagreements were felt in the heavy atmosphere rather than witnessed or heard.

I found this insistence on authenticity and openness both exhilarating and scary. I feel things strongly and deeply and don't fully trust any verbal expression. I want to sit with my thoughts and feelings for a long time before expressing them. It takes me time to get round to communicating what I feel or think.

During my school years I often found myself getting into trouble innocently and so began to feel I needed to hide. One time in primary school myself and Johnny Walker had stayed on after final bell, playing as 10-year-olds do. We climbed some of the drainpipes for fun. Unknown to us the drainpipe we ascended gave us a view into the teacher's toilet. An angry Miss Penny, a formidable spinster, accused us of sexual misdemeanors, perving into her most private space. Again in my secondary school I chanced upon some friends barring a classroom door and restraining another boy who I had never met before. We joined in this lad's discomfort. At school assembly the next day, the assistant rector called out my name along with other friends as hooligans of the worst kind because of these actions . We then had to report for six of the best from his feared Assistant Rector Mr O'Neill whilst the Rector, Dr Lee, watched on in calm repose. These and other incidents developed in me a reticence to show my true self. Yet it was so refreshing to be myself and to speak openly.

The 1970s Calvinist culture in Glasgow generally frowned on anything colourful, emotional, or sexual. This culture was being forced open by the permissive culture of the 1960s and 1970s. There was a real thirst for change in the air, especially amongst the youth culture. In the late 1970s the punk culture burst on to the scene with a refreshing, devil may care, iconoclastic attitude, that was fed up with the dreaming of the hippies and wanted change and authenticity now. It distrusted the establishment. Was bored with the plastic dreams of economic progress, as many of us languished on the dole without a job or a career. There seemed no future. The razzamatazz of the Queen's Silver Jubilee was lost on you if you were signing on for £20 a week. All this youthful energy could congeal and putrify into sickly apathy, or turn into an anarchic, mindless violence.

Or…….These guys at the Buddhist Centre were working together. They had come across something that resonated with their own idealism, vision and longing for something that mattered.

To me it was very attractive. Listening to Sangharakshita, it was clear that the man had spiritual depth. Going along to Heruka I could see that these guys were involved in something radical. I thought I might find a way here to resolve my own existential situation and move through the pain and grief of becoming paraplegic. I certainly felt that I needed something. I really enjoyed being around these Buddhists and was intrigued by it all.

It was still very early days in the establishing of Buddhism in the West. There was a lot of 'academic' Buddhism, which amounted to not much more than the occasional philosophical discussion about the serious affairs of life. FWBO was trying to create a community of friends practising deeply together. I soon came to know that Ajita, Dhammarati, Vairocana, and Danavira lived together as a Buddhist community; alongwith some other young guys.

They were all quite a rather motley crew. Motley, in that they were all different and brought their different personalities to the table. They were a crew in that they worked together to run the Buddhist Centre.

I was intrigued to hear of their adventures further afield than Glasgow, hitchhiking down to London and Norwich for Buddhist weekends. This was a new world. I had heard of hitchhiking in songs and in films. Here were guys who actually travelled this way. Adventuring off to other parts of the UK that involved meeting a host of different lives on the way. Car drivers, lorry drivers. Straight people, curious people. Other free spirits. Lonely travelling salesman. The sexually frustrated on the make. Other free spirits. Worlds were opening up for me. They were hitchhiking to Buddhist events. Meeting others in the Buddhist Order. Going on meditation retreats. Being on seminar with Sangharakshita. And they would return buzzed up - inspired by new teachings, by more ideas about how to live creatively, with fresh insights into the spiritual life and how to practice it.

These stories really sparked my imagination and I was keen to have some Buddhist adventures of my own. I did not have to wait long as there was to be an FWBO Men's Convention in April 1979 at Vinehall School in Surrey. I had heard the Order Members talk about the Order convention there the year before, and I wanted to taste some of this for myself.

Heading South again

So once again I headed south. This time I drove. I had realised after becoming wheelchair user that learning to drive was going to be necessary. Up until breaking my back I had resisted driving and owning a car, as I was concerned about the environmental impact car pollution was having on the planet. But public transport in the 1970s was not accessible to wheelchairs users. Buses were out of the question. If you could get on a train it was usually to travel in the guard's van along with the various parcels that were en route to delivery. It was cold, noisy, and rather humiliating to travel without any comfort and treated like baggage. I had quickly learned in Phillipshill spinal unit that driving a car would be the only real solution to travelling around. I had seen the odd-looking, blue, three wheelers that disabled people drove. And I was not looking forward to this stigmatisation. Luckily for me the Government had just introduced a mobility allowance for disabled people, and I could use this to lease a car of my own rather than get one of the blue three wheelers.

My first car

Following my discharge from hospital In January 1977 I had taken driving lessons and, after a few months, passed my test first time. My aunt had connections with the Glasgow trades house charity and they had granted me £1500 to buy a car. I would need an automatic gear box and have hand controls fitted for the brake and accelerator. There were few automatics on the market, but there was one that I liked. I picked up a blue Mark I Escort estate from the Arnold Clark garage on Dalmarnock Road. It was just within my budget. That car would take me many places.

In April a few of us loaded up this car, piled in and off on Buddhist convention we went. First stop, however, was Croydon. There were a couple of young men who had left Glasgow to live in Aryatara community in Purley, Croydon. We had arranged with them to stay in the community overnight. In those days FWBO communities regularly hosted travellers from other FWBO centres who were visiting or just passing through. As we were on our way to the Vinehall event we were made welcome. There were some Buddhist businesses run from the community: a gardening business and the Secret Garden Cafe. I was keen to see just what a Buddhist business looked like. Next morning we sought out the cafe which was rather tucked away. The Secret Garden Cafe was small, and sat next to the Croydon bus station. I remember it being furnished with some basic chairs and tables and a blackboard behind the counter announcing the vegetarian menu. It had the feel to it of an alternative world backed by youthful Ideals if not much finance. We had some food there, then made our way on to Vinehall which was near Hastings.

Vinehall School was built in 1838 and was set in six and 47 acres of parkland that included football pitches and woodland. To me it seemed a bit run down and rambling. We had our program of morning meditation, study groups, talks and Puja - a devotional practice with chanting. In many ways I found this first experience of retreat outside the Glasgow Sangha a bit overwhelming. It wasn't easy for me to connect with others. I was still very shy, and I must have been dealing with many issues of my recent disability, as well as the impact of meeting many new people. However, I do have a few memories.

I remember going for a push in the woodland on my own and meeting an order member called Ananda. We got talking and discovered that we both worked in accounting. I found him very approachable and was pleased to be able to connect with him. I learned that Ananda also wrote poetry and had been one of the first order members ordained by Sangharakshita in 1968.

Another memory is of meeting an Irish order member called Mangala. In our conversation he said to me "You're looking a bit sorry for yourself, buck yourself up". This was pretty direct and quite normal for the open communication of those times. And it did have the effect of pulling me out of my mood.

I also recall a group of guys going out to a local church. This was not long after Sangharakshita had published 'Buddhism and Blasphemy.' - a response to the famous blasphemy trial of 1977. To free oneself of our fear of a controlling Old Testament God, cathartic blasphemy could be useful. Some of the visitors had felt the need to express their views on Christianity and record them in the church's visitor book. On return to Vinehall they had regretted this and hurried back to try and retrieve the situation, only to find that the vicar had already spotted their blasphemous remarks. This incident didn't reflect very well on us, or our attempts to leave our Christian heritage behind.

I have very positive memories of Sangharakshita leading meditations in the large hall that we used as a shrine room. The stillness, depth, and luminosity of these meditations I can recall today. These sorts of experiences really helped me develop trust in meditation and in Sangharakshita as my teacher.

Graduation

Meanwhile as I was having these great adventures I was still finishing my BSc. I had lost interest in following a career and was really just finishing the course without much motivation. I had considered dropping out the course, but thought it best to finish what I had started. I passed my final exams and graduated that summer. It did not mean much to me, but it did to my parents. Both my mum and dad were very proud of me. They were very pleased to attend the graduation ceremony that was to be held in the old Fruit Market building in Candleriggs. It does not sound very grand but the fruit market had moved out of town to Blochairn and the old fruit market had been converted into a venue for music et cetera. It had kept all of it's period charm, including a lofty vaulted roof of cast iron columns and balconies. It was located in the old Merchant City quarter and was a short five minute walk south of Strathclyde University. There would be over 1000 people graduating students and their families there for the event. We had to book our graduation gowns and photographers and go through all the preparation for the big day. Both my parents and my aunt Isobel came to witness the spectacle. My aunt had played a big part in helping me get back to university and was very proud of me. It was through her connection with an old boss of hers that I had got the grant to purchase my car and get the hand controls fitted. All the graduates had to climb a set of wooden steps onto the stage to receive their degree certificate from the University Chancellor, on the stage they would be ceremonially awarded their degree, a BSc in my case. There was a lot of pomp and ceremony to the event. Due to the steps I would not be able to ascend to the stage. The Chancellor would make his way down the steps after all the degrees were awarded and confirm my title in front of the stage. The time came and he made his descent, I wheeled from my position to meet him. An almighty cheer and spontaneous handclapping seemed to go up from all those attending, much to my embarrassment. I was generally quite shy and reticent in those days and so was deeply discomfited by this sign of appreciation. Using a wheelchair I felt I stood out enough, and this was unwelcome attention.

I felt a bit disconnected with all this appreciation. I supposed the other students and families wanted to show their appreciation, for all the adversity I had overcome. I felt very awkward. The graduation photograph afterwards shows an almost resentful look on my face. I really did not want to be seen as the super cripple.

The University course was over and I did not have either further studies or job to go to. During the so-called 'Milk Run' when graduates apply for their future jobs, I had been unsure whether I would carry on and do an honours year. My tutors were keen for me to do Honours. In the end I decided that I had had enough of University life and wanted to move on. But I had no interest in following a career. The only thing that seemed meaningful and interested me, was Buddhism. This late decision left me a bit high and dry, without a job to go to. My aunt managed to arrange an interview with one of the leading accounting firms in the city. I attended, possibly with my mum. The firm's partner who held the interview told me that this year's intake of graduates had already happened and there was no place for me in his firm. He then went on to politely mention that although I now had a degree, it was not that special, and I should seriously hunt for a job. Good for him - no pity there, which was refreshing although sobering.

I hunted the job market and although I could not get a position to train as a chartered accountant, I did get into a firm in Mitchell Street as a trainee tax accountant. It was a grand, old, Victorian red sandstone building with a street level entrance which made it wheelchair accessible. Then there was a lift up to the first floor offices. There was also a Doorman on hand to open the door and welcome visitors, and he was willing to help me in any way that was needed. It was an office of maybe 20 employees or so. And it was a shock to find myself the lucky recipient of this job. It was a good job with stablility, and financially rewarding prospects. There were many other trainees in the company. Some had completed one year of study exams and training. Others two years! And yet others who had just sat, and passed their final exams to be fully qualified tax accountants. The dress code in the office was shirt, tie, and suit. I wore the woolen suit I still had from my time at Coats Patons. It was rather stylish I thought. A pale coloured, off white, with a slight grey green mottle to it. It was definitely not pinstripe, dark grey, or black. And if I looked around the large office it was all pinstripe or dark coloured suits that met my gaze. With a dark tie. And as you looked at the complexions and faces of the accountants there, you noticed that the new recruits still had a fresh complexion. But it seemed that the longer you worked there and the more exams you passed, the more the colour would drain from you until you were left with a rather grey and pasty look. Whether it was the lack of sunlight in the office, or the stress of the job, or the effects of willing yourself into the constrictions of being a tax accountant, the result of working here year in and year out seemed to drain the colour out of you.

The other trainees testified to the long hours that you needed to devote to study in the evenings after finishing a day's work, if you were to pass the arduous exams. The benefit of all this effort was a stable and financially rewarding job. If you put all of yourself into it then you would have a job, and an above average salary. The cost to yourself would be a life time of rather dull work that sucked the vitality out of you.

My second retreat – Loch Sunart

That summer of graduation also saw me turn 21 and, legally anyway, reach my full adulthood. Although It did not seem to me that I was an adult. I still felt that I was searching for meaning in life and looking to make my way in the world. I had found something of meaning in my teacher Sangharakshita, and then there were my developing friendships in FWBO, but it was just a start. I probably had a party to mark this traditional coming of age, but I do not remember. I do remember Gair having his 21st birthday party at one of the basement bars we used to drink in. It was paid for by mum and dad and they popped in for a short time. The music stopped and they said a few words to mark his birthday and celebrate his birthday. After that the music, drinking and dancing continued until the early hours.

I probably had something similar, the memories are lost to me. What I do remember is the birthday present I got from my parents. It was a light grey coloured sleeping bag with synthetic insulation. It was one of the new cocoon shaped bags, which meant it was narrow at the feet and broad at the shoulders, with an integral hood that encircled your head. You could pull the hood's drawcord tight so that only your face was exposed to the elements. Maximum coverage whilst still allowing yourself the chance to breathe easily.

Mum and I went to the mountaineering shop at the eastern end of the great Western Road to get this high-tech bit of kit. When I went on retreat, I had been using an old sleeping bag from my scouting days. Most of the places we used were pretty old and draughty so having a warm comfortable sleeping bag was important. So for my 21st birthday I invested in this good bit of kit. It probably cost £30, which would be £100 in today's money. It was warm and compact and lasted me for many years.

The Glasgow Buddhist Centre summer retreat was near Strontian by Loch Sunart in Ardnamurchan. Again led by Ajita. There were some people who came up from Croydon this time. There was a keen lively young man who seemed a bit naïve, with a mercurial nature and an order member called Virabhadra who was studying to be a doctor. Virabhadra's longterm plan was to go to India to help with the poor Dalit people and bring them much needed healthcare. He was a very kind, gentle man with dark hair and a round face; at times he exuded a cheeky good humoured laugh. I liked him and we seemed to get on well.

I remember meditating a lot in the shrine room at the back of the house. I was keen in those days to experience deep bliss in my meditation and remember doing whatever I could to have blissful meditations. Others on the retreat where talking about the blissful experiences they were having in meditation. Derek and I felt I we were missing out a bit. Another Order member present was Siddhiratna from London. He worked as a graphic designer and seemed very left-wing in his politics. He was reading the Dharma bums by Jack Kerouac. Gair and I had both read this the year before. Siddhiratna and I talked about the novel and about the sense of freedom that it invoked.

The retreat was set in a remote part of Scotland that I had never been to before. It was a four hour drive, including a short trip on the Corran ferry across Loch Linnhe. In those days we would hire a remote cottage or hunting Lodge recommended by a letting agency we had got to know; they knew the sort of quiet places that we were looking for. And in this way, we would end up travelling to remote areas in the West Highlands for retreats. Going to these places I got to know some beautiful parts of the country and learn a bit about them. Strontian is gaelic for 'point of the fairies' and is a little village on the sea loch of loch Sunart. It's major claim to fame is that it has an element of the periodical table named after it. In 1790 French prisoners of war working in the lead mine, to provide shot for the British war effort, found something else apart from the lead they were looking for. It turned out to be a completely new element and was named strontia after the village.

There was a weekend retreat booked for the weekend following my first week at the tax accountants this retreat was held that Grey Craigs. An old WW II underwater listening post, now an outdoor centre on the north-west coast of the Isle of Cumbrae. For many Glaswegians the island is known as Millport, the name of its largest town lying on the southern coast. From Glasgow you drive 38 miles south-west to Largs, then take the short ferry trip to the island, head north once you come off the ferry for 10 miles and you find the low buildings of Grey Craigs.

Danavira, Sangharatna, and Dipankara were ordained hear by Sangharakshita in 1976. Ajita told me the story of how he and Sangharakshita had travelled to this ordination retreat together. They had got to Largs and found that there was a bit of a storm raging across the Firth of the Clyde. This meant that the crossing to Cumbrae was in doubt. Ajita recalled to me standing beside Sangharakshita and feeling him willing the captain of the ferry to make the trip. Instilling the captain with confidence to brave the choppy waters of the Firth. In the end the ferry sailed and the ordinations of Danavira, Sangharatna, and Dipankara went ahead.

So here we were again on retreat 'doon the water' at Grey Craigs. 'Doon the water' being Glaswegian slang for any spot below Glasgow on the Firth of Clyde. The term denies the beauty of the firth and its landscape. The River Clyde broadens out to be 26 miles at widest point of the Firth, and is more sea than river. The Firth is protected from the Atlantic Ocean by a long stretch of land known as the Kintyre Peninsula. In the Firth are many other peninsulas and islands. Gare Loch, Loch Long, Loch Fyne all lead off from the waters of the Firth. To the north of the island you can see Ben Lomond and the Arrochar Alps, to the west the Paps of Jura and Knapdale are visible. Another beautiful location to be on retreat. Even if the buildings were spartan and slightly militaristic.

I left for Grey Craigs after finishing work in the tax Accountants, arriving late on Friday evening along with Brian who also had to leave after work. The program included meditation, Puja, communication exercises and study around the theme of right livelihood.

During the course of the weekend we explored ideas around right livelihood. I was particularly inspired by the possibility of working with other Buddhists and our cooperative way. I remember also the communication exercises that we did.

Communication exercises had been devised as a way of learning about communication, and especially the non-verbal dimensions to it. I was paired up with Brian. Brian was about the same age as me, perhaps a year older. He was below average height, with sandy coloured hair, and very muscular. What I noticed above all else was the tremendous energy that radiated off him. We sat in front of each other, perhaps a foot or two apart. In the first part we were to rest our gaze on the person in front of us and not just look at them, but really take them in and feel for them as another human being just like us.

I understood what I was being asked to do, and it seemed like a good idea. But to meet the intense gaze coming from those blue eyes, and feeling that intense dynamism coming my way in seismic waves, meant it was not comfortable or easy to sit there meeting Brian's gaze. It was something like a two man encounter group, no holds barred. Nothing getting in the way. Sitting there as a tsunami broke and flowed over me. I remember those communication exercises. I remember feeling incredibly blocked and wooden in the face of so much life.

The Spartan simplicity of the accommodation was made bearable by being with such an interesting bunch and by going out for walks in the mild weather along by the shore. I had to use the road because of my wheelchair. But there were few cars to disturb the beauty, and the road wound its way close to the rocky shoreline.

As I wheeled along the road, I pondered on my job situation. I had just been presented with the idealism of working in a cooperative work situation with other Buddhist friends. And here I was working in Tax Accountants office. One situation offered security and good money. The other offered basic financial support and lots of risk. One offered the richness of doing meaningful work with friends. The other offered routine, mechanical, lifesapping work. The staff in the tax office were grey suited and grey complexioned, they seemed to lose lifeforce the longer they worked there. My Buddhist friends where young, alive, radical and informed about life. Not surprisingly, but summoning up all my confidence, I chose the latter.

On the Monday morning after the retreat I drove into work as normal. Arriving at the office I asked to see my boss. I steeled myself. I wheeled into his room for the interview. I told him that I had realised that this job was just not for me. I told him I was leaving. We agreed that I should leave immediately which suited me just perfectly. I left his office, left the building and never looked back.

Right Livelihood – Ink Print & Design

My Buddhist friends had been running a printing business based in a near derelict building at the bottom of Hope Street, just across from Central Station, called Ink, Print, and Design. I wanted to be a part of this.

It was Dhammarati who had designed the meditation poster that originally attracted me to the Buddhist Centre. He had been designing these silkscreen A1 size posters at the Glasgow Print Studios. It was clear that he was a very talented designer. The Glasgow public would wait for new meditation posters to be fly posted on walls and hoardings before taking them down as prizes to be put up in their own bedrooms, along with their posters of Che Guevara. There was one series of posters entitled. 'Buddhism for Heroes'. The first one depicted Lauren Bacal in a stunningly beautiful pose, with her smouldering look, pouting away as the ultimate femme fatale, robbing men of their sanity. Another poster had Humphrey Bogart as the archetypal moody male. Fedora pulled down over soft eyes. And a gaze that spoke of knowing and seeing things clearly, unfazed, with an impassive look on his face.

On the back of Dhammarati's design flair a silk screen printing business started. They had to move out of the non-profitmaking print studios as too much commercial work came in for the non-profit making Print Studios. Hence the move to 21 Hope Street.

It was a fledgeling business in those days and struggling for work. Ink print and design was well known amongst the left-wing and alternative circles. It was on the first floor, reached by what had been a grand staircase. None of the other rooms on the first floor were occupied. All the two or three floors above were also unoccupied. The building closely resembled the water logged building from the climactic scene in the 1982 movie Blade Runner starring Harrison Ford in a dystopian future. There was no toilet in our premises. I had to enter the offices next door and wheel round to the back of the building where there was a functioning toilet. However, at various times burglars had stolen the lead from the roof and this caused plenty of water damage from the rain. This water damage had penetrated the plaster ceilings of the floors above us and had brought them down. So to get to the toilet I had to wheel over the fallen plaster debris that had once been a ceiling. It never occurred to me to ask for it to be cleared, even though progress to the toilet was difficult and my wheels carried plenty of plaster dust back into our office.

Originally it was thought that I could help out with the accounts of the business and do some photography work in the dark room. But I was way too naive to bring some financial order to the business. Three years studying accounts at Strathclyde University in a far too perfect environment gave me little sense of what I could do to bring financial order to this situation. After a few months it was clear that it was impractical for me to work at Ink and I left.

I had really enjoyed being in the creative environment of design and print. The world of visual art was completely new to me and I was excited to see the graphic designers create beautiful graphics from scratch. Dhammarati was the main designer, but there was also Bob Gammie, who had been trained in graphic design. Bob was able to pass on to Dhammarati many of the skills he had learnt. As well as posters for the Buddhist Centre we were doing more commercial work such as leaflets, brochures, business cards for local businesses, and bands such as Travis and Goodbye Mr McKenzie.

Heruka – Men's Community

Not long after the Grey Craigs retreat I asked to move into the community that lived at the centre. I think that I had quite quickly realised that if I was to really get much out of my connection with FWDO and Buddhism then I needed to get close to the heart of it. So far, I had been going along to weekly classes and to weekend and longer retreats. I could see that those who lived in the community had a greater depth of friendship and communication with each other, and that their life and practice was more intense.

I saw that the community members really knew each other from living together. They shared their lives and their inspirations. Each member was quite different from another, and by living together there was rub and sparks flew, and there was commitment to go beyond personal differences to create a community that worked. Living together brought about intense communication that seemed fuller and closer – people really got to know each other.

Housing and My Family Home

At this time, in the summer of 79, I was still living in the family home with my parents and three brothers. My elder sister had got married are few years previously and now lived in Cairneyhill in Fife. After graduation Fiona now worked as a PE teacher. My family home was originally in Kings Park in Glasgow's South Side. The famous Hamden Park football ground was close enough for us to be able to judge how the football games were going by the tenor and timbre of the roars that rumbled our way.

Kings Park was a relatively recent suburb of Glasgow and had been built on open countryside until the 1920s. The developers had included a variety of housing in the development from sandstone bungalows, semi-detached homes, through to the cheaper four in a block cottage flats that we stayed in. It was a lovely area to grow up. There were many open spaces and fields to play and explore. Kings Park is surrounded by the working class areas of Toryglen, Cathcart, Croftoot and Rutherglen. Our house in Montford Avenue was very close to Toryglen.

The house in Montford had three or four steps leading up from the pavement to the pathway that led to the front door where there were another couple of steps leading into our house. Since breaking my back in August '76, I used a wheelchair. No matter how we explored possible ways of putting ramps to the front door it was not going to be possible. The house would remain inaccessible for me as a wheelchair user. So when I came out of Phillips Hill Hospital in January 1977, after six months of recuperation and rehabilitation as a wheelchair user, it was clear that the family house would not suit me.

For the next year or so I was dependent on one of my brothers or my father to get up or down these steps that led to our front door. Once inside I could manage unassisted. Our part of Montford Avenue was up a steep Hill which also did not help getting out and about.

My parents decided that they needed to sell the house. This was a huge sacrifice. They had invested in the big dream of owning their own home and they were very proud and happy with 173 Montford Avenue. It had worked well as a home for five children. The primary school was a 15 minute walk away, mainly through the big field as all the locals call it, but officially known as 100 acre Hill. There were shops nearby. Many other families with young children were living in our street. Every house had its own garden and there were plenty of trees and green spaces for kids to explore and play in.. And there was a good bus service into the city centre. It was a good area to raise a family.

The three bedroomed house was a bit cramped as three brothers sometimes shared the same bedroom, using bunkbeds. But this was not unusual for working class Glasgow where whole families sometimes shared a single end. A single end had a recess bed, store and eating area all in one room. My aunt Maisie and uncle Don had something like this. One weekend we stayed with them and our cousin Margaret. Four or five of us shared the one bed, only possible because we slept head to toe.

Mum and dad had always done whatever they could for us. Making sure we got a good start in life, whether it was a good education or healthy food, so in a way it came as no surprise that they decided to move from Montford.

The search for a suitable accessible home had begun whilst I was still in the spinal unit at Phillips Hill Hospital. Our social worker had to come out to see the house and assess its suitability for a wheelchair user. Once I got inside everything was fine. All the doors were wide enough for a wheelchair to pass through, and the bathroom was spacious enough to be used easily. The problem was the two sets of steps and the hill the house was built on. These two problems meant that even with the front garden, there would not be big enough space to install a ramp to the front door.

So began a search for a suitable new home. Mum went along to the surgery of our local MP. Teddy Taylor was an intelligent fast talking bundle of energy - he got things done for his constituents. He backed us with our approach to Glasgow city housing department. Teddy Taylor was a mover and shaker.

This was in the early days of disability awareness. In the late 1870's few buildings and homes had been built with the needs of wheelchair users in mind. Homes that were suitable for a wheelchair user were few and far between. And so we went on the housing list expecting a long wait and a hard search.

In the meantime, until a suitable home was allocated, we had to make do at Montford Avenue. I say we because I was dependent on help from Robin, Duncan, Gair or my dad to get me down the steps to get out, and then needed one of them to pull me up the steps to return back in. And all this had to be pre-arranged and planned, as the mobile phone was still to be invented! Luckily, they were all fit so it wasn't too difficult for one of them to pull me up or down the steps. But it was a hugely inhibiting factor in my daily life. Thankfully they were always willing to help and were very generous in that way towards me.

Before I had broken my back, I had been saving money to be able to afford a flat on my own in my first year at university. I had worked a few evenings each week in an off-sales selling alcohol. This money had gone into my bank account to realise the dream of my own flat. I was a young man and felt somewhat constrained living still with my parents. Some of my own friends already had their own place. Not only was I feeling the constriction of still living with my parents and under their authority but I couldn't enter and return the house whenever I wanted.

My parents had been very kind to me. They hadn't asked me for any part of my £30 a week student grant to go towards rent food or electricity. Young men want their independence and freedom. Young men want to be free of their parents influence and control. They strain and pull at parental restraints. And I was no different. I had wanted the freedom of my own place.

After about a year of looking for a suitable house, a place became available in Langside. This was not too far away from Kings Park. So we went to see the new place and it turned out to be a large ground floor flat in a sandstone terrace. It was in a broad, quiet road near to the Victoria infirmary: the largest hospital in Glasgow's south side. There was a very small garden between the terrace and the pavement. There was one step into the close that could easily be ramped from the pavement. Cartside Street is in a very flat part of the city so that was a plus, whereas Kings Park is fairly hilly and not so suitable to push around in a wheelchair. When we went inside, we saw that the flat was in quite a state of disrepair and would need quite a bit of work done to it. The electrics needed upgrading, the floorboards needed attention, and the whole flat would need to carpeted and decorated.

This was the first real possibility we had seen. So although there was all this internal work to do, we decided to take the offer. The flat was in a street of newer terraced houses, surrounded by streets of older traditional red sandstone houses. It had a sense of being part of an older community. And I liked that quality of community.

There were three steps down to the communal back garden, and because of the arrangement of the back steps it would not be possible to install a ramp to give me access. The garden had a bin area, and then a 20 foot lawn with some flower borders. Beyond the end of the garden, past the metal railings, was a grassy area with a pathway and beyond this public stretch of grass flowed the White Cart, a small river about 3 metres wide. On the other side of the river was the large car park for Scottish Power bordered by a large open field where Weirs, a local engineering company had a sports ground. There was a long public footpath that went along the edge of the White Cart and meant that there was a lot of greenery around.

Wheelchair Accessible Accommodation

The neighbours we met on those first viewings seemed friendly. It was in a spacious pleasant part of Glasgow that, like Kings Park, had good transport links and roads. It was clear that the flat itself would work for us after some refurbishment. So we signed the lease and plans to move began to take shape.

Refurbishing 102 Cartside Street

First, the city council housing department put in a ramp at the front from the pavement to the close entrance, and then a sliding door on the refitted bathroom. Then my dad began his renovation work to rewire all the electrics and then decorate. My youngest brother Duncan helped my dad a lot on the renovation. I was quite envious of the time Duncan spent with my dad re-wiring the old electrics and sorting various other bits and pieces. I had never really had much time with my father since I was about six when I can remember a day trip by train down to the coast with him and my elder sister. His long working hours and regular six- or seven-day working week meant he was often absent, or tired. I was envious of Duncan being shown how to wire the electrics of the house and how to saw and lay floorboards. It was a particularly dirty job, especially when he had to get under the floorboards and thread the electric cable from one room to another. Although I was envious of Duncan, I'm not sure it was a very pleasant job for him. He certainly didn't feel I had anything to be jealous of. But for me it was this time working with my Dad in his area of expertise that I envied. Like a passport into my father's world.

In time the flat was renovated and decorated and we moved in. This was a great relief to me as I could now come and go as I pleased. And I could enjoy wheeling along the White Cart pathway to Langside and Queens Park.

The flat itself had a single bedroom, double bedroom, large bedroom, lounge, small kitchen and a bathroom. Gair, Robin and I moved into the large bedroom; mum and dad had the adjacent double bedroom; Duncan had the single bedroom by the front door to himself.

So now, a couple of years since breaking my back, life was getting back on track. I was getting used to life from a wheelchair, I had an accessible home and I had my blue Escort estate to travel around in.

Parents

As I look back on these developments I am so struck by the continuing generosity of my parents. They just responded to what I needed. They sold the family home that they were so proud to own for my benefit. My dad worked extra hours in the new flat, at the end of long work days, to get everything ready. The whole family was moved to Cartside Street for my benefit. And this is what they had done all our life. Their sons and daughter meant so much to them. Everything was geared around the children to give us all we needed. Both my parents worked to bring enough money in for our needs and so we could go to school until we were ready to go on to university or college. Education was something that my parents really valued, in a very typical Scottish working class way. My dad had had to leave school at 14 and wasn't permitted to stay on to get a good education. His foster parents decided he would leave as soon as he could to bring extra money into the croft. He became a joiner's apprentice at 14. Even although the headmaster pleaded for him to be allowed to stay on and to pass his exams and further his education. He was seen to be very intelligent and could have gone on to a good education. His foster parents went against the pleas the headmaster. At 14 years old, and while still a young teenager, he was sent out to work to bring in a much needed income. My mum also left school as soon as she could in order to help financially at home.

My parents had met in London towards the end of the war. They had met at Scottish country dancing. They had got married in London and my sister was born there after some years of trying for a family. My mum's first pregnancy was stillborn and buried with much sorrow. A few years later Fiona was born. And they were so pleased to be able to start a family. When mum was pregnant with my elder brother they moved back to Glasgow and lodged with my grandparents in the east end in Appin Road while they were saving the deposit for their own home. My brother Gair was born shortly after they returned to Glasgow. I followed a year after Gair, and in another two years Robin was born, then another two years and Duncan followed. They were very thankful to have a family and wanted the best for us, and gave whatever was needed for us to grow up well. My father never drank. His two needs where his cigarettes, he smoked 60 Benson and Hedges a day, and he always had a weekly bottle of lemonade and bottle of coca cola. Likewise with my mother, she never spent much money on herself for clothes or shoes. She also smoked, but less than my father, maybe around 20 a day.

One Sunday morning I heard whisperings from my parent' bedroom and sensed a heavy atmosphere in the home. My parents were disagreeing - dad had been a Communist in his early 20s and was now still very much a socialist. He supported the Labour party's introduction of secondary modern schools. My mother was more pragmatic and always wanted the best for her children. They were arguing over what secondary schools their children should go to. My dad wanted us to go to the local secondary modern school. My mother wanted us to take advantage of the grant system run by the local Labour city council that enabled bright kids from working-class families to attend prestigious fee-paying schools. Both of them wanted the best for us, they were just disagreeing on what the best was. In the end my mother got her way and Gair, Robin and I, went to Glasgow High School. "Just remember "she would say constantly to us "There is nobody better than you.". My father could be quite harsh on us, without him really realising this. And my mother was regularly softening some of this harshness. My father once made me a cricket bat for my seventh birthday which I was really pleased with. It was made of cherry wood. I couldn't wait to play with it. That afternoon I played with Gair and Robin and of course I was using the bat, hitting the balls bowled with great gusto and dexterity. However, the plants in the borders planted by our upstairs neighbour, Mrs Waugh, suffered greatly at my match winning shots and my mum called a halt on the match. Then on my dad's return from work he heard how I had savaged not only the fast bowling of my brothers but also the neighbour's flowers. In an angry fit he took the cherished new birthday present and placed it on the coal fire to be consumed in the flames. And that was that - I needed to learn a lesson.

Mum regularly reminded us that dad was really very kind, but since he had grown up without caring parents, he did not always know what he was doing. As a young kid I was really sad that I only had one set of grandparents, whereas my friends had two. I felt really sorry for my dad.

In those authoritarian times in Glasgow the mother was the sweeter of the two parents, and when it came to really laying down the law or getting the slipper as punishment it was dad who stepped up. Mostly it was the father who became the authority figure. It was the father that teenage sons rebelled against. In a way my dad never stood a chance. His lack of sensitivity alienated him from us. His Highland upbringing was so different from Glasgow. He was usually tired and grumpy with us kids when he wasn't working. He hadn't really built much rapport with us. So when there were four brothers entering into the testosterone confusion of adolescence, rebelling against any perceived unjust authority, my dad was prime target. As our strength and energy peaked, he struggled to control us. We all clashed with him. I think Gair, the eldest, especially so. There was even a brief fight between them in our new hallway. My father came off second best in the tussle when Gair head-butted him and my father collapsed to the floor.

Leaving Home

My parents had done all they could for me. They had provided a solid platform for me to launch myself into life from. They had encouraged to me to be independent, were maybe even a bit concerned how I could still live a full life as a wheelchair user. I felt I needed to leave home. I had already stayed too long. To move forward in my Buddhist life it seemed I needed to live in the community. So after just over a year and a half I left 102 Cartside Street to join the men's community 'Heruka'.

I moved out one Saturday. I packed a lot of my belongings into my own car. Mum and dad put bedding and other things into dad's Lada, and drove them over from our home in Cartside Street to the community in Kelvinside Terrace South. At the other end they carried my belongings up the stairs into the community.

I was to share a room with Dhammarati. He had kindly made space amid the artistic clutter of his room for me to put a single mattress down on the carpeted floor. The space was enough for me. I'm sure my parents must've been happy that I was leaving home and still independent, and also more than a little concerned at the level of home comforts offered in the community.

13 Kelvinside Terrace South became my new address. I moved from the south side to the West End. The West End was where Glasgow University was located, so lots of student flats and bedsits. There where Pakistani shops open to the wee small hours where you could snack on samosas and pakoras, a new Indian delicacy now available in Glasgow. The oldest Indian restaurants in the city were in the West End. We had the Sheesh Mahal in Park Road and the Koh-I-Noor in Gibson Street. The Koh I Noor later relocated to North Street after an attempt to extend the premises by taking away a load bearing wall lead to the buildings collapse. The drinking hostelries on nearby Byers Road were renowned student hangouts. For a greener time, you could take a walk in the Botanic Gardens and visit the Kibble Palace greenhouse to see exotic plants from across the globe and luxuriate in the warm spaces they grew in. The architecture of Kelvinside and Hyndland boasted some of the grandest houses in the city, including Great Western Terrace designed by the famous Glasgow architect Alexander 'Greek' Thomson. In the 1970s Glasgow's West End carried the torch of wealth, Bohemia and academia for Glaswegians.

It was here in the West End of the city that the men's community was housed. A friend to one of the Order Members was in a bit of a predicament. He was a follower of Bhagwan Sri Rajneesh whose ashram was in Pune, India at this time. This Glaswegian sanyassin had been instructed to return to the ashram as soon as he could. So he was in need of raising the necessary funds to be able to follow his Guru's wishes. Without much money in the bank he had to resort to selling his only current collateral, a flat in the West End. Dhammarati and Vairocana were both working at the time,. Dhammarati as a mental health nurse and Vairocana as a fireman. Between them they were able to get a joint mortgage for £10,000. There had been previous communities rented in Bath Street and Nithsdale Road. This one would be owned by FWBO Glasgow and sizeable enough and well situated to double up as a Buddhist Centre. It's purchase in 1976 heralded the beginning of a vibrant and inspired period in FWBO Glasgow's history. Classes were very popular there, with up to 70 people attending and Buddhism established itself on the Glasgow alternative map. The community was named 'Heruka' by Sangharakshita alluding to the wild and free nature of the Glasgow Order Members.

13 Kelvinside South

Heruka is on the third floor of a West End sandstone terrace building. It faces south, and in front of it are green parkland and trees leading steeply down to the river Kelvin. It is a 10 minute walk to the Botanic Gardens and Byers Road. A broad stairway leads up from the street to the close entrance. From there stairs lead upward to the other two floors. These stairs are also broad with a dog leg turn at the landing halfway between floors, here on the landing light streams into the close from a large window.

Each of these old Edwardian flats are protected by tall storm doors at their individual entrance, before you come to the real front door. Stepping through the front door you find abroad hallway three or 4 yards wide that runs the length of the flat.

The first door on the left enters into a large room with two windows looking south, these windows run from close to the floor all the way to the ceiling and let in a lot of light. It has a deep brown shag carpet that has seen better days. There is a shrine facing you with a beautiful Burmese Buddha in earth touching mudra. Behind the Buddha the wall is brightly decorated with a Tibetan style mural.

The second room on the left is also very large but only has one window. This room is a double bedroom.

The third on the left room is even bigger than the previous two, and also has a very high ceiling. The windows almost span the entire space of the South facing wall. To the right is a large closed fireplace. The room is decorated gaudily in red, white, blue and yellow primary colours.

Coming out of the lounge and turning sharply to your left around the corner you are met by shoes and a row of coats and jackets on hooks. As you go around to your right you find yourself in the kitchen. Below the north facing window which gives you a view of the back close and the backs of the houses of Kelvinside Terrace North there is a sink and a small draining board. The cooker is just to the left of the window. Along the length of the kitchen is a low, dark stained table with two long benches either side to sit on. Behind you there are louvre doors that give access to a small shower room below and a large storage space above.

Coming out of the kitchen you find a small bedroom that faces out over the back close. It is big enough only to have a single bed.

Next to that small bedroom is a larger bedroom big enough for two people to share.

The last bedroom next to the bathroom is just slightly smaller, but big enough for two to share.

The bathroom has a small step up into it. On the right as you go in as a deep metal bath, but you have to squeeze by a gas fired heated towel rail to get to the toilet and the sink.

The community has its own cat, a ginger tabby, called appropriately enough Ginger. Ginger's diet is yellow, he will eat anything yellow. He eats custard, sweet corn, cheddar cheese, and cornflakes with milk. That is what he lives on mostly, although he probably supplements this diet with the mice he can catch outside in the back courts or down by the river.

Going Forth

It was a 6 mile journey from Cartside Street over to the community in Kelvinside Terrace. I drove with my Ford Escort full of some essential clothing and my record collection. In my father's green Lada is the duvet and other bedding that I will need. The route took us up Sinclair Drive, past the Victoria Infirmary and the wall where I had glimpsed the meditation poster that was turning out to be a window to my future. Then we went along Prospect Hill Road, Cathcart Road the old Gorbals onto The new Kingston Bridge that took us high over the River Clyde with views of the city centre and also West past the wasted docklands of the Broomielaw and away further Kilpatrick hills.

Coming off the bridge the road drops down into the underpass that slashes through the city centre past The Mitchell Library before resurfacing at Charing Cross. Then on through Saint

Georges Cross where my aunt Maisie had lived. Although now there is nothing left of the tenement building or whole community where she had lived. Once we got onto great Western Road we were beginning to emerge into the west end. Great Western Road runs straight for miles to Anniesland, undulating as it rises over the braes of Hillhead and Kelvinside. It is a wide road flanked by the typical red sandstone terraced houses four stories high. Once over the bridge at Park Road you have entered the West End proper. To get to the community you have to turn right at the Botanic Gardens, pass the BBC on your right, over the river Kelvin, before heading up the steep short hill to Kelvinside terrace.

A journey that took us 30 minutes had been decided by years of longing to leave home. It is said that the Buddha-to-be left home in the still of the night, taking some last looks at his beautiful wife and the son he named Rahula, fetter. His heart longing for a greater beauty than was on offer in the Gilded Palace his father had created for him, where every known sensual pleasure was entertained.

My own parents hadn't created such a pleasure palace. They had created a home from the best that working class parents knew of, the best of their culture. As a child it was plenty for me, as a youth I had begun to strain for my own independence. My parents had moved to Cartside Street to allow me my physical independence. A young man kicks and pushes against authority and hierarchy to fight for his own autonomy and individuality. Somewhere I dimly sensed this process, while still raging against my father. I felt the Pathos of the physical struggles between my brother and father that left the elder man weaker on the floor. And I needed to get out. My mother told me how she loved us too much to compensate for the lack of my father. She moved so much more in the world of feeling than I could sense or understand. Her attentions were too much for the adolescent me. I couldn't understand her forgiving nature and how some situations would not get to her. I was annoyed and upset by the lack of justice in the world, an abstraction that didn't touch her though she would care for elderly neighbours and friends in poor health.

I felt constricted by my father's authority at home and felt I was having to follow my parents' rules. I felt suffocated under the close emotional blood ties of my family. Looking back, I can see that I had been well provided for by my parents. My family felt progressive and open in comparison to some of my friends. It seemed that we had a more intelligent, forward to looking attitude to life. Yet it wasn't enough. I still felt bound. I had to go.

Living in the Community

I was to share a room with Dhammarati. This was the bedroom two doors down on the right, looking out over the back courts. He had prepared for my arrival by clearing a space on the floor where I could fit my single mattress, just beside a set of freestanding metal shelves that he used to store a lot of his art materials. It didn't take us too long to carry my belongings up the stairs to the flat. My past and my future were together that afternoon as my family helped me move into the community. I had seen that the way forward in my life was to live with these other Buddhist men in the community.

Aryamitra and Brian shared the bedroom next to the bathroom. Aryamitra had recently moved up to Glasgow from London. He had worked in the printing business that had been based in London in the basement of the LBC but was now in Glasgow. Windhorse Press had printed the FWBO Newsletter and Mitrata (a training booklet for those more involved in FWBO). Somehow or other a deal had been struck whereby Windhorse Press moved to Glasgow and became part of Windhorse Wholefoods. The original idea for a Buddhist Right Livelihood business in Glasgow had been to start a wholefood shop. But it had proved difficult to find suitable premises and, in the meantime, based on Dhammarati's skill as a graphic designer, a printing business had been started. Dhammarati had been designing posters to advertise the Buddhist Centre and clearly had a huge talent as a designer. His posters were not only very effective in promoting the centre but very sought after as 'the' poster to have on your bedroom wall. The posters were fly-posted around the city and as soon as they went up, they were removed to grace many a bedsit wall. Aryamitra came to be in Glasgow on account of the merger between a graphics business and a printing business. He was a very warm and friendly man. Aryamitra had been taught yoga by the famous BKS Iyengar in Pune, India and taught classes in Glasgow. Brian had been manager of the Nevis Sport mountain equipment shop in Sauchiehall Street. One day staff had alerted him that there were two suspected shoplifters in the store. Ajita and Danavira were larking around by pretending to steal bulky sleeping bags, and sticking them up their jumpers. Seeing that the staff were a bit paranoid about them being shoplifters, Ajita and Danavira played up to their misconceptions. Brian saw what was going on immediately and relaxed the other staff. A couple of weeks later Brian had come along to learn to meditate at the Buddhist Centre and was pleasantly surprised to be taught to meditate by the two so called 'shoplifters'. Brian was a second Dan in Shotokan karate as well as a talented mountaineer who was planning an ascent of Everest.

Paul and Joss shared a large bedroom. Paul and I were contemporaries; both coming along around the same time. Both had finished our degrees that summer. Joss was a sturdily built, young, public school Englishman with dark hair, and a cocky twinkle in his eye. Joss managed the gardening business. Paul, myself, Brian and Joss were in our early 20s. While Aryamitra, Dhammarati, Danavira and the Ajita were in their early 30s. Susiddhi was a bit older and in his mid 30s.

Daily routine

There weren't many rules in the community. But there was a strong vision to the community. At 7am there was chanting followed by an hour and a half of meditation. Then breakfast together, which usually consisted of cornflakes or muesli followed by toast. Some preferred the healthier option of muesli, others had the ubiquitous corn flakes, which since they were yellow were also enjoyed by Ginger the cat.

After breakfast we went our separate ways. Dhammarati and Aryamitra went off to work in the printing business Ink, Print and Design. Joss, Brian and Paul were the core of Gardening Friends. The gardening team were very distinctive in their red boiler suits. These were the two quite separate co-operative businesses run under the name of Windhorse Wholefoods Ltd. Neither were remotely concerned with wholefoods, it just so happened that there were skills available to start these businesses. All over FWBO the form of business adopted was the worker's co-operative as this legal entity most closely matched the vision of Buddhists working together. It did cause some confusion, because we were not strictly speaking a co-operative in that we wanted the committed Buddhists to be in control of the spiritual direction of the business. But it was the best legal structure for our businesses we could find. Throughout FWBO our co-operatives adopted the name 'Windhorse' as this symbol was seen as embodying the energy needed to take our Buddhist Vision out into the world.

Susiddhi, Ajita and Danavira were very involved in running the Buddhist Centre and various other FWBO activities.

I wasn't working and would spend my day in various ways.

We all took our turn in preparing the evening vegetarian meal. Ajita in particular cooked an excellent curry, Dahl and rice. I soon soon mastered the art of cooking curry from the raw spices but not before a few hiccups. My first meal using garlic had the whole bulb thrown in without any peeling. Another had been so hot it was almost inedible. The food was all vegetarian which was fine for me as I had been vegetarian since the first winter retreat that I had been on. Where Ajita was a master at cooking curry, Susiddhi had two simple dishes he would cook-one of them being quiche the other a lentil pie. And he wasn't very fond of vegetables which was something to behold in a vegetarian!

Closed Community and Friendship

The community had recently become a closed community, which meant that girlfriends were not allowed to stay overnight. Before I had moved in there had been some great parties; one of the community had spent the night tucked away in the bed space above the shower with his lover. This bed space opened directly onto the kitchen. Order member and lover bounding down in the morning to eat a hearty breakfast with the other community members.

The idea of the closed community was to help intensify and deepen friendship and communication between us. We had seen that men often relied on women to emotionally nurture them. Part of becoming a true man lay in developing one's feminine side. Homophobia was a significant issue in 1970s and 1980s Glasgow and this prevented most men from developing emotionally close connections with other men. Deep male friendship was a rarity. Many men could easily talk about what they thought with their mates in a blokey manner. Tenderness and affection were reserved solely for girlfriends. This was a time when Sangharakshita was trying to get a Buddhist movement to be so much more than a weekly hobby. More than just something you did at your Buddhist class once a week. He talked about the True Individual and inspired many of us to move beyond the gender roles dictated by the habits of society. We followed in the footsteps of CG Jung and his individuation process and were developing and integrating our so-called 'feminine' side. By not having girlfriends stay over we hoped communication could become more tender, emotional, and intimate. There was a culture developing in FWBO of men being openly physically affectionate with each other. This was a shocking challenge to most of the stiff upper lip brigade, and in its own way helped men to connect openly.

OPENNESS

Openness was a quality highly prized by us. We knew how rife hypocrisy was and looked to undermine it through complete openness. The hippy mindset of good vibes and positive energy permeated the hippy culture we moved in. People sincerely spoke like the 'Oddball' character in the popular film 'Kelly's Heroes' and wished to transform the stultified atmosphere of our society. In our verve to be open nothing was to be hidden; nothing we did, or thought, no sexual proclivities, no bodily function, was deemed inappropriate for communal discourse. In this way many barriers were dissolved and fears lifted. As a community we decided not to lock the bathroom door while using the toilet - for us this was a small step in freeing us from certain taboos. In small ways like this many perceived barriers were broken through and fears dissolved.

In our naivete, many necessary emotional defenses were assaulted inappropriately. But nothing was to be allowed to block the free flow of our energy. In our imitation of Tantric Buddhism, nothing should be allowed to block energy. In our desire to break through to openness this was highly valued.

Common Purse

This openness was fiscal as well as emotional and we experimented with a common purse where all our money was shared equally. Everybody took the same support to live on, not wages, to promote commonality and the integrity of the community. So although I wasn't working, I lived on the same as others, by putting the extra money I got from disability benefits into the community common purse.

One of the benefits, for me, of this sharing was that I was able to borrow Brian's camera to shoot a couple of rolls of photographs. I had never owned a camera or used one. My father owned one but it had never occurred to me to borrow his. So for a couple of days I wandered down by the river Kelvin, and along the river walkway, taking photos. And I saw the river and its surroundings with an aesthetic sense. I decided to use one roll of black and white film as I thought it would be more atmospheric. I enjoyed this and when the prints came back from the developer, I was pleased to see my shots of community members and the riverbank had come out pretty well for a first timer.

Living in the community meant that I heard a lot more casual communication than before. It was a very social way of living, surrounded by many other young men. And I would hear news of what was happening at other centres and about the characters involved there.

In these early, formative, days of FWBO, Sangharakshita would regularly hold seminars. He would invite a dozen men or women from different UK centres and study a Buddhist text with them. Sometimes it would be something that had just been translated and published. Discussion would not be restricted to the text but would range to all of the hot issues of the day. This could include simple courtesies of community living - remembering to tell other community members that you were going out and when you would return. As a group of young men, we were not necessarily that switched on in matters of courtesy and being aware of how to live with others. We were young and idealistic and not always very mature.

Around this time ideas and practices around the single sex ideal were formulating. Many of us in FWBO were finding a lot of benefit in living, working, and going on retreat with members of the same sex. This separation of the genders wasn't to everyone's taste. It certainly seemed to be encouraged by Sangharakshita. Articles about the importance of young men leaving home were written and discussed. Views about the relative aptitude of men and women to follow the spiritual life were developing. This was the women men and angels period. It was slightly comforting as a man to be told some of these views. But then I'd look around at the women I knew, in my family and friends, and see that there were some very impressive women. Some of whom were clearly more together than me, so this view did not hold up in my own experience. In fact it was discomfiting and debilitating to think that I was less of a man because I could see women more together than me!

I'd always had trouble in my teens with what it meant to be a man. The model of the Glasgow macho male was not attractive to me as it seemed far too harsh. Yet the energy and vibrancy of many Glaswegian men showed me something I felt I lacked. My own relationship with my father was minimal and didn't offer much guidance. There was a bleakness growing up in the austerity of the late 1950s and early 1960s. The model for the typical male was to be strong and rational; and the female was expected to be sweet and emotional. I wanted something much more colourful. It was so much more interesting to explore the fluidity of David Bowie's 'gender bending', or Mark Bolan's 'Glam Rock'. There seemed a gulf between the sexes. The single sex ideal seemed to me to be a way to bridge this gap. To become complete as a human being, a man who felt and thought.

Disability and sexuality

For me another complicating factor was my disability. One of the hardest things to come to terms with, was the way I was treated because I sat in a wheelchair. I now tended to get a lot of pity and sympathy from certain types of women. Other types just ruled me out as a sexual partner, I wasn't even on their radar! I was getting quite used to these responses. One Saturday night Gair and I had gone out to the Strathclyde University Student Union. There was a band playing; maybe Steve Hillage or Magazine. I don't remember which. After the gig we were downing drinks in the bar.

In walked a drop dead gorgeous blonde girl. She came over to me and we talked a little. She was very pretty, and lovely to talk to, if just a little drunk. Then without any warning she began to kiss me. I didn't resist! We kissed for a while. Then she had to leave. But before leaving she was adamant that we should meet again on the coming Monday at 1 PM outside her flat in Royal Exchange Square. This was a really up market address in the town centre. I knew she was inebriated, and was probably just acting out of the drink. But I agreed to meet her. My better sense thinking that she would probably have forgotten her drunken escapade by the morning. And that she had taken pity on the poor disabled boy. I thought it was unlikely she would show, but she had been adamant. And she was very pretty. So...

I turned up, on time, at the address and waited. She didn't show and my worst expectations proved correct. But I hung about a bit, just in case. At twenty past one, an expensive car pulled up and my blonde got out! Then someone who could have been her sister, and an older man, probably her father. They started to unload some domestic goods, and take them in the doorway to the upstairs flats. She never looked around to find her hot date. I was not on her mind. I left disheartened and downbeat about my chances of finding a girlfriend who didn't pity me.

My own relationship to sexuality wasn't straightforward. I still felt horny and attracted to girls but my disability complicated things. Yes I could still get an erection, but ejaculation was problematic, even after a long period of stimulation. And not able to physically thrust my hips due to my paralysis - I didn't feel I was able to be the dominant male partner that my culture told me I should be. Due to my paralysis I had limited control over my bladder and bowels, and was very worried that I would have a mishap during sex. I wouldn't have been able to live with that! As a young disabled man my relations with women were fraught with all sorts of issues.

Conscious of all these issues it seemed a good idea to sort out my identity, my confidence, and become a bit more emotionally mature before venturing into relationships again. If I could sort out some of these issues in the relative safety of a men's environment then I could return to dating.

A lot of my friends were getting married and having kids. I wasn't really interested in either of these two projects. And without much chance of a career, I didn't feel I could financially support a marriage anyway.

But I did want to sort myself out and that is what I prioritised.

Some of my community friends were dabbling in homosexual encounters to free themselves of the homophobic fear of male intimacy. I declined the opportunity. There was already enough for me to deal with. It's not that I hadn't felt drawn to men, I had. One of the men back in the Gairloch hotel I worked in one summer, was very camp. One day I had to go to his caravan with a message. I found him naked under the bed covers with one of the female staff. He was nonchalantly at ease, in what seemed like a post-coitus bed. He heard the message I brought. And then flirted with me outrageously and suggestively. Teasing me to join their antics in the bed. I was excited. But too naive and unsure to do anything about it, and left.

Being disabled, with the issues that brought up. Having grown up in a sexually repressed Calvinistic culture. That seemed to be enough to get on with. I thought I'd try other ways to liberate my sexuality.

To be continued…